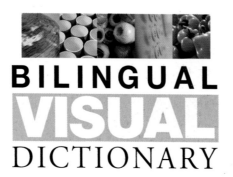

BILINGUAL
VISUAL
DICTIONARY

BILINGUAL
VISUAL
DICTIONARY

London, New York, Melbourne, Munich, Delhi

Senior Editor Angela Wilkes
Project Art Editor Katie Eke
Production Editor Luca Frassinetti
Production Controller Linda Dare
Managing Art Editor Lee Griffiths
Managing Editor Stephanie Farrrow
US Editor Jill Hamilton

Designed for Dorling Kindersley by WaltonCreative.com
Art Editor Colin Walton, assisted by Tracy Musson
Designers Peter Radcliffe, Earl Neish, Ann Cannings
Picture Research Marissa Keating

**Language content for Dorling Kindersley by
g-and-w PUBLISHING
Managed by** Jane Wightwick
Translation by Kazumi Honda
Layout by Mark Wightwick
Editing by Cheryl Hutty

First American Edition, 2011

Published in the United States by DK Publishing,
345 Hudson Street, New York, New York 10014

10 9 8 7
019—179043—May/2011

Published in Great Britain by Dorling Kindersley Limited.

A catalog record for this book is available from
the Library of Congress.

ISBN 978-0-7566-7556-1

DK books are available at special discounts when purchased in bulk
for sales promotions, premiums, fund-raising, or educational use. For
details, contact: DK Publishing Special Markets, 345 Hudson Street,
New York, New York 10014 or SpecialSales@dk.com

Printed and bound in China by L. Rex Printing Co. Ltd.

Discover more at
www.dk.com

目次 mokuji
contents

42
健康
kenkō
health

146
外食
gaishoku
eating out

252
娯楽
goraku
leisure

人 hito • people

外観 gaikan • appearance

健康 kenkō • health

家庭 katei • home

職務 shokumu • services

買い物 kaimono • shopping

食べ物 tabemono • food

外食 gaishoku • eating out

学習 gakushū • study

仕事 shigoto • work

交通 kōtsū • transportation

スポーツ supōtsu • sports

娯楽 goraku • leisure

環境 kankyō • environment

参考資料 sankō shiryō • reference

この辞典について

情報の理解と記憶に視覚的資料が効果的なことは、既に実証されています。その原理に従って図版を主体に作成された本和英ビジュアル辞典は、広範な分野の実用的現代用語を収録しています。

内容はテーマ別に分けられ、レストラン、ジム、家庭や職場から、動物界や宇宙に至るまで、日常社会のほとんどの分野が詳細に網羅されています。さらに会話と語彙の拡大に役立てられるよう、関連用語や便利な言い回しも付け加えられています。

実用的で使いやすく、見ておもしろい本辞典は、日本語に関心のある方に欠かせない参考資料です。

表記法について
本辞典には、日本で一般に使われている漢字仮名まじり表記が使用されています。魚の名前など、漢字でも仮名でも表記できる言葉は、発音ガイドとして載せたローマ字から仮名の綴りが分かるため、漢字の方を使うようにしました。

発音ガイドには、日本語の学習者なら大抵知っているローマ字が使われています。ローマ字の表記法にはいくつかありますが、本書ではもっとも発音しやすいと思われる方法を選びました。なお、長音は母音の上に長音記号をつけて表記しています。

単語はすべて、次のように漢字・仮名、ローマ字、英語の順で掲載しています。

昼食	**旅券**
chūshoku	ryoken
lunch	**passport**

動詞は英語の後に (v) をつけて示しています。

収穫する shūkaku suru | **harvest (v)**

辞典の後ろには和英別の索引があり、ローマ字または英語で引きたい言葉を調べ、該当する図が載っているページを探すことができます。漢字・仮名の書き方を調べる場合は、先ずローマ字または英語の索引を調べ、該当するページをご覧ください。

about the dictionary

The use of pictures is proven to aid understanding and the retention of information. Working on this principle, this highly illustrated English–Japanese bilingual dictionary presents a large range of useful current vocabulary.

The dictionary is divided thematically and covers most aspects of the everyday world in detail, from the restaurant to the gym, the home to the workplace, outer space to the animal kingdom. You will also find additional words and phrases for conversational use and for extending your vocabulary.

This is an essential reference tool for anyone interested in languages—practical, stimulating, and easy-to-use.

A few things to note

The three different writing systems of the Japanese script (*Kanji*, *Katakana*, and *Hiragana*) are employed in the dictionary following common usage. However, when alternative usages exist for individual items of vocabulary (for example animals), we have usually chosen to use Kanji since the pronunciation that follows will indicate the Katakana or Hiragana spellings.

The pronunciation included for the Japanese is shown in *Romaji*, the romanization system that is familiar to most learners of Japanese (see Pronunciation tips).

The entries are always presented in the same order—Japanese, Romaji, English:

昼食	**旅券**
chūshoku	ryoken
lunch	**passport**

Verbs are indicated by a **(v)** after the English, for example:

収穫する shūkaku suru | **harvest (v)**

Each language also has its own index at the back of the book. Here you can look up a word in either English or Romaji and be referred to the page number(s) where it appears. To reference the Japanese characters, look up a word either in the Romaji or English index and then go to the page indicated.

Pronunciation tips
The pronunciation in the dictionary is shown in the Romaji system. There are some variations possible in Romaji, but we have tried to use the most user-friendly transcription.

Many of the letters used in Romaji can be pronounced as they would be in English, but some require special explanation:

r	Never rolled; pronounced with the tip of the tongue against the gum of the upper front teeth
f	Pronounced more with the lips and less with the teeth than its English equivalent
w	A semi-vowel pronounced with slack lips
ts	As in "pits"
ei	As in "pay" or "rein"
n/m	The Japanese characters ん and ン are generally pronounced "n" as in さん san, but this changes to "m" before the sounds "b" or "p", e.g. コンピュータ kompyūta.

Japanese vowels are pronounced short similar to the English "pat/pet/pit/pot/put". However, they can also be lengthened. This is shown in the Japanese script by a dash (ー) and in the Romaji by a macron (flat line) over the vowel (ū). Lengthened vowels should have the sound sustained for approximately twice the amount of time.

In general, Japanese words do not have a particular stress, or emphasis. Each syllable is stressed roughly equally. Take care also to pronounce the syllables separately; there are no "silent" letters. For example, カフェ kafe is pronounced "ka-fay" rather than "kayf."

この辞典の使い方

仕事や趣味、海外旅行の準備で初めて日本語を習う方でも、あるいは既に日本語を知っていて語彙を伸ばしたい方でも、本書は大切な学習ツールとして様々な方法で使うことができます。

　初心者の方は、同語源語（外来語など異なる言語で語源が共通する言葉）や派生語（同一言語で語源が共通する言葉）に注目すると語彙の習得に便利です。また、こうした学習によって、異なる言語が互いに影響しあっていることも分かってくるでしょう。たとえば日本語には英語圏から流入した食物関連の言葉が多くありますが、一方、日本から英語圏へ流出した技術や大衆文化に関する言葉も多くあります。

実用的な学習方法

• 自宅、職場、学校や大学の構内を歩いているとき、辞典の該当するページを見てみましょう。そして辞典を閉じ、周りを見回して、名前をいえるものがいくつあるか見てみましょう。

• 単語カードを作り、表に英語、裏に漢字や仮名、ローマ字で日本語を書きましょう。単語カードは常に持ち歩き、頻繁に自分でテストしてみましょう。一回テストが終わったら、次のテストの前にカードを入れ替えましょう。

• 特定のページに載っている単語をできるだけたくさん使い、短い物語、手紙、会話文などを書いてみましょう。これは語彙を記憶し、書き方を覚えるのに役立ちます。長い文章を書いてみたい場合は、一つの文に単語を2～3語使ってみましょう。

• 視覚的記憶に強い方は、紙に図を描くか写し、辞典を閉じて、図の下に単語を書いてみましょう。

• 自信がついてきたら、ローマ字索引から単語を選択し、該当ページの図を見る前に、その意味を覚えているかどうかチェックしましょう。

how to use this book

Whether you are learning a new language for business, pleasure, or in preparation for a vacation abroad, or are hoping to extend your vocabulary in an already familiar language, this dictionary is a valuable learning tool that you can use in a number of different ways.

　When learning a new language, look out for cognates (words that are alike in different languages) and derivations (words that share a common root in a particular language). You can also see where the languages have influenced each other. For example, English has imported some terms for food from Japanese but, in turn, has exported many terms used in technology and popular culture.

Practical learning activities

• As you move around your home, workplace, or college, try looking at the pages which cover that setting. You could then close the book, look around you and see how many of the objects and features you can name.

• Make flashcards for yourself with English on one side and Japanese/Romaji on the other side. Carry the cards with you and test yourself frequently, making sure you shuffle them between each test.

• Challenge yourself to write a story, letter, or dialogue using as many of the terms on a particular page as possible. This will help you retain the vocabulary and remember the spelling. If you want to build up to writing a longer text, start with sentences incorporating 2–3 words.

• If you have a very visual memory, try drawing or tracing items from the book onto a piece of paper, then close the book and fill in the words below the picture.

• Once you are more confident, pick out words in the foreign language index and see if you know what they mean before turning to the relevant page to check if you were right.

人 hito
people

身体 karada • body

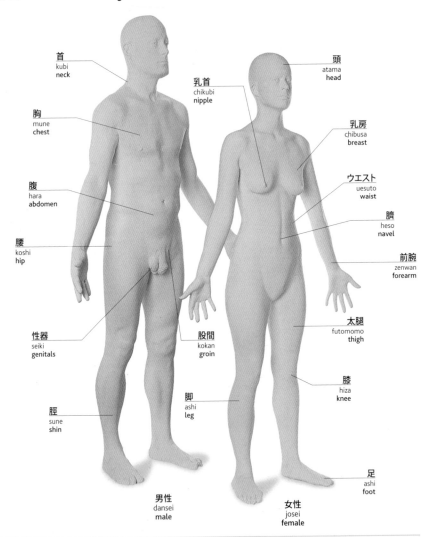

首
kubi
neck

頭
atama
head

乳首
chikubi
nipple

胸
mune
chest

乳房
chibusa
breast

ウエスト
uesuto
waist

腹
hara
abdomen

臍
heso
navel

腰
koshi
hip

前腕
zenwan
forearm

性器
seiki
genitals

股間
kokan
groin

太腿
futomomo
thigh

膝
hiza
knee

脛
sune
shin

脚
ashi
leg

足
ashi
foot

男性
dansei
male

女性
josei
female

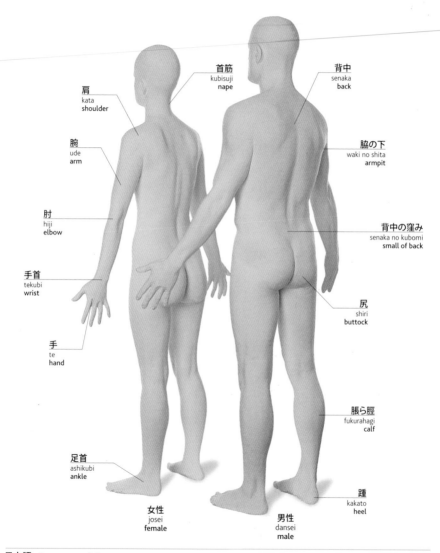

首筋
kubisuji
nape

肩
kata
shoulder

背中
senaka
back

腕
ude
arm

脇の下
waki no shita
armpit

肘
hiji
elbow

背中の窪み
senaka no kubomi
small of back

手首
tekubi
wrist

尻
shiri
buttock

手
te
hand

脹ら脛
fukurahagi
calf

足首
ashikubi
ankle

踵
kakato
heel

女性
josei
female

男性
dansei
male

顔 kao • face

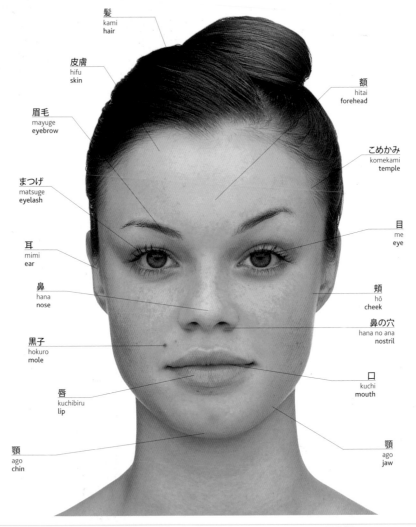

髪
kami
hair

皮膚
hifu
skin

眉毛
mayuge
eyebrow

まつげ
matsuge
eyelash

耳
mimi
ear

鼻
hana
nose

黒子
hokuro
mole

唇
kuchibiru
lip

顎
ago
chin

額
hitai
forehead

こめかみ
komekami
temple

目
me
eye

頬
hō
cheek

鼻の穴
hana no ana
nostril

口
kuchi
mouth

顎
ago
jaw

皮
shiwa
wrinkle

そばかす
sobakasu
freckle

毛穴
keana
pore

えくぼ
ekubo
dimple

手 te • hand

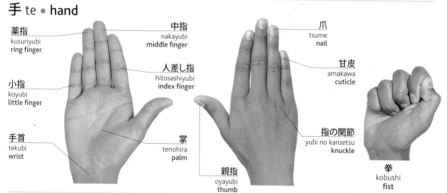

薬指
kusuriyubi
ring finger

中指
nakayubi
middle finger

爪
tsume
nail

人差し指
hitosashiyubi
index finger

甘皮
amakawa
cuticle

小指
koyubi
little finger

手首
tekubi
wrist

掌
tenohira
palm

指の関節
yubi no kansetsu
knuckle

親指
oyayubi
thumb

拳
kobushi
fist

足 ashi • foot

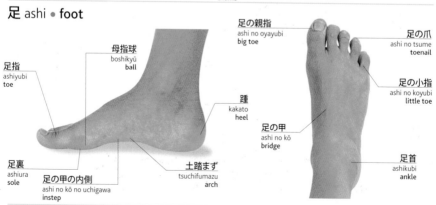

母指球
boshikyū
ball

足の親指
ashi no oyayubi
big toe

足の爪
ashi no tsume
toenail

足指
ashiyubi
toe

踵
kakato
heel

足の小指
ashi no koyubi
little toe

足の甲
ashi no kō
bridge

足裏
ashiura
sole

足の甲の内側
ashi no kō no uchigawa
instep

土踏まず
tsuchifumazu
arch

足首
ashikubi
ankle

筋肉 kinniku • muscles

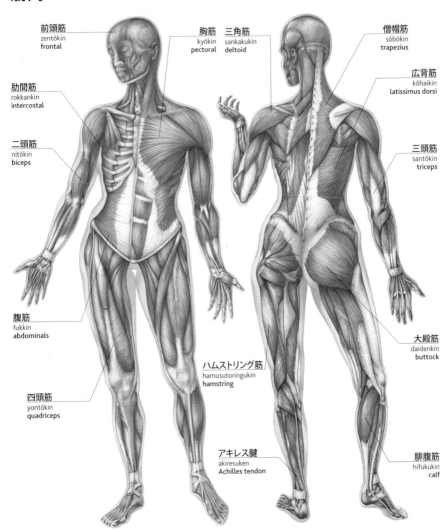

前頭筋
zentōkin
frontal

胸筋
kyōkin
pectoral

三角筋
sankakukin
deltoid

僧帽筋
sōbōkin
trapezius

肋間筋
rokkankin
intercostal

広背筋
kōhaikin
latissimus dorsi

二頭筋
nitōkin
biceps

三頭筋
santōkin
triceps

腹筋
fukkin
abdominals

大殿筋
daidenkin
buttock

ハムストリング筋
hamusutoringukin
hamstring

四頭筋
yontōkin
quadriceps

アキレス腱
akiresuken
Achilles tendon

腓腹筋
hifukukin
calf

骨格 kokkaku • skeleton

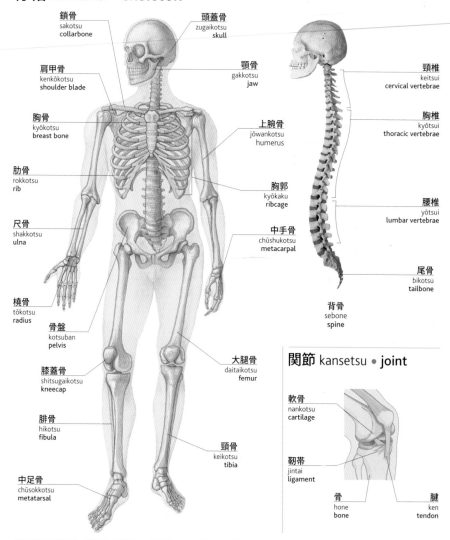

鎖骨
sakotsu
collarbone

頭蓋骨
zugaikotsu
skull

頸骨
gakkotsu
jaw

肩甲骨
kenkōkotsu
shoulder blade

胸骨
kyōkotsu
breast bone

肋骨
rokkotsu
rib

尺骨
shakkotsu
ulna

橈骨
tōkotsu
radius

骨盤
kotsuban
pelvis

膝蓋骨
shitsugaikotsu
kneecap

腓骨
hikotsu
fibula

中足骨
chūsokkotsu
metatarsal

上腕骨
jōwankotsu
humerus

胸郭
kyōkaku
ribcage

中手骨
chūshukotsu
metacarpal

大腿骨
daitaikotsu
femur

頸骨
keikotsu
tibia

頸椎
keitsui
cervical vertebrae

胸椎
kyōtsui
thoracic vertebrae

腰椎
yōtsui
lumbar vertebrae

尾骨
bikotsu
tailbone

背骨
sebone
spine

関節 kansetsu • joint

軟骨
nankotsu
cartilage

靭帯
jintai
ligament

骨
hone
bone

腱
ken
tendon

内蔵 naizō • internal organs

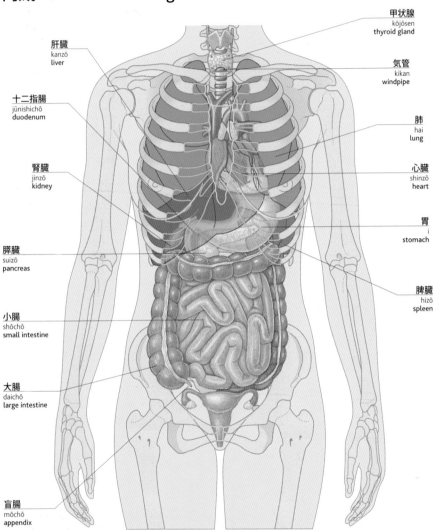

甲状腺
kōjōsen
thyroid gland

気管
kikan
windpipe

肝臓
kanzō
liver

十二指腸
jūnishichō
duodenum

肺
hai
lung

腎臓
jinzō
kidney

心臓
shinzō
heart

胃
i
stomach

膵臓
suizō
pancreas

脾臓
hizō
spleen

小腸
shōchō
small intestine

大腸
daichō
large intestine

盲腸
mōchō
appendix

頭 atama • head

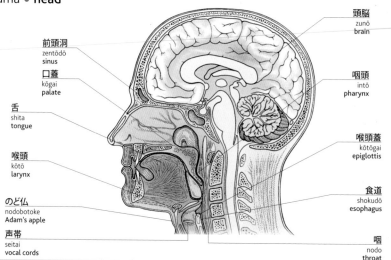

頭脳
zunō
brain

前頭洞
zentōdō
sinus

口蓋
kōgai
palate

舌
shita
tongue

喉頭
kōtō
larynx

のど仏
nodobotoke
Adam's apple

声帯
seitai
vocal cords

咽頭
intō
pharynx

喉頭蓋
kōtōgai
epiglottis

食道
shokudō
esophagus

咽
nodo
throat

人体系統 jintai keitō • body systems

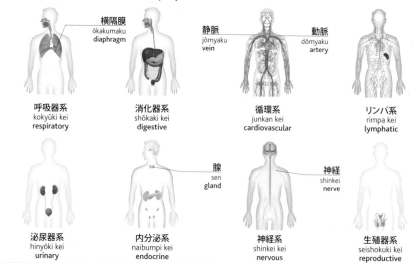

横隔膜
ōkakumaku
diaphragm

静脈
jōmyaku
vein

動脈
dōmyaku
artery

呼吸器系
kokyūki kei
respiratory

消化器系
shōkaki kei
digestive

循環系
junkan kei
cardiovascular

リンパ系
rimpa kei
lymphatic

腺
sen
gland

神経
shinkei
nerve

泌尿器系
hinyōki kei
urinary

内分泌系
naibumpi kei
endocrine

神経系
shinkei kei
nervous

生殖器系
seishokuki kei
reproductive

生殖器 seishokuki • reproductive organs

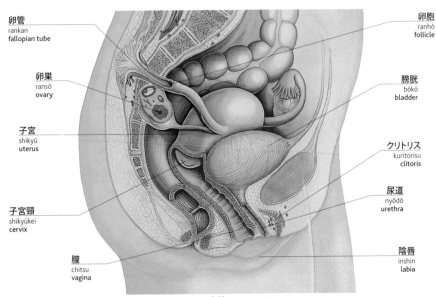

卵管 rankan fallopian tube	卵胞 ranhō follicle
卵巣 ransō ovary	膀胱 bōkō bladder
子宮 shikyū uterus	クリトリス kuritorisu clitoris
	尿道 nyōdō urethra
子宮頸 shikyūkei cervix	
膣 chitsu vagina	陰唇 inshin labia

女性 josei | female

生殖 seishoku • reproduction

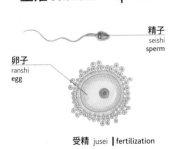

精子
seishi
sperm

卵子
ranshi
egg

受精 jusei | fertilization

関連用語 kanrenyōgo • vocabulary

ホルモン horumon hormone	不能症 funōshō impotent	妊娠できる ninshin dekiru fertile
排卵 hairan ovulation	妊娠する ninshin suru conceive	月経 gekkei menstruation
不妊症 funinshō infertile	性交 seikō intercourse	性感染症 sei kansenshō sexually transmitted disease

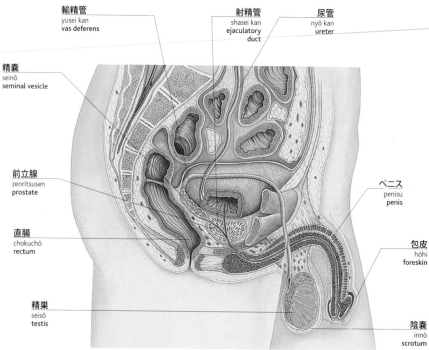

輪精管
yusei kan
vas deferens

射精管
shasei kan
**ejaculatory
duct**

尿管
nyō kan
ureter

精囊
seinō
seminal vesicle

前立腺
zenritsusen
prostate

ペニス
penisu
penis

直腸
chokuchō
rectum

包皮
hōhi
foreskin

精巣
seisō
testis

陰嚢
innō
scrotum

男性 dansei | **male**

避妊 hinin • **contraception**

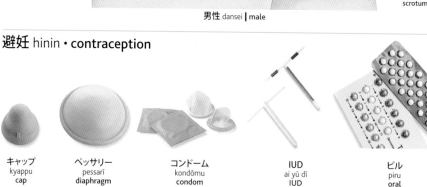

キャップ
kyappu
cap

ペッサリー
pessarī
diaphragm

コンドーム
kondōmu
condom

IUD
ai yū dī
IUD

ピル
piru
**oral
contraceptives**

家族 kazoku • family

祖母
sobo
grandmother

祖父
sofu
grandfather

叔父/伯父
oji
uncle (older/younger)

叔母/伯母
oba
aunt (older/younger)

父
chichi
father

母
haha
mother

従兄弟
itoko
cousin

兄弟
kyōdai
brother

姉妹
shimai
sister

妻
tsuma
wife

嫁
yome
daughter-in-law

息子
musuko
son

娘
musume
daughter

婿
muko
son-in-law

孫息子
mago musuko
grandson

孫娘
mago musume
granddaughter

夫
otto
husband

関連用語 kanrenyōgo • vocabulary

親類 shinrui relatives	両親 ryōshin parents	孫 mago grandchildren	継母 mama haha stepmother	継息子 mama musuko stepson	配偶者 haigūsha partner
世代 sedai generation	子供 kodomo children	祖父母 sofubo grandparents	継父 mama chichi stepfather	継娘 mama musume stepdaughter	双子 futago twins

成長段階 seichō dankai • stages

義母
gibo
mother-in-law

義父
gifu
father-in-law

義兄弟
gikyōdai
brother-in-law

義理の姉妹
giri no shimai
sister-in-law

姪
mei
niece

甥
oi
nephew

乳児
nyūji
baby

子供
kodomo
child

男の子
otoko no ko
boy

女の子
onna no ko
girl

ティーンエージャー
tīn'ējā
teenager

大人
otona
adult

男性
dansei
man

女性
josei
woman

敬称 keishō • titles

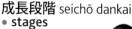

さん
san
Mrs.

さん
san
Mr.

ちゃん
chan
Miss/Master

人間関係 ningen kankei • relationships

マネージャー
manējā
manager

アシスタント
ashisutanto
assistant

ビジネス・パートナー
bijinesu pātonā
business partner

雇用主
koyōnushi
employer

従業員
jūgyōin
employee

同僚
dōryō
colleague

オフィス ofisu | **office**

隣人
rinjin
neighbor

友人
yūjin
friend

知人
chijin
acquaintance

ペンパル
pemparu
pen pal

ボーイフレンド
bōifurendo
boyfriend

ガールフレンド
gārufurendo
girlfriend

婚約者
kon'yakusha
fiancé

婚約者
kon'yakusha
fiancée

カップル kappuru | **couple**

婚約中のカップル kon'yaku-chū no kappuru | **engaged couple**

感情 kanjō • emotions

微笑
bishō
smile

嬉しい
ureshī
happy

悲しい
kanashī
sad

興奮する
kōfun suru
excited

飽きる
akiru
bored

驚く
odoroku
surprised

怖がる
kowagaru
scared

しか目面
shikame-zura
frown

怒る
okoru
angry

混乱する
konran suru
confused

心配する
shimpai suru
worried

不安
fuan
nervous

誇る
hokoru
proud

自信
jishin
confident

恥ずかしい
hazukashī
embarrassed

はにかむ
hanikamu
shy

関連用語 kanrenyōgo • vocabulary

狼狽する rōbai suru **upset**	笑う warau **laugh (v)**	溜息をつく tameiki o tsuku **sigh (v)**	怒鳴る donaru **shout (v)**
衝撃を受ける shōgeki o ukeru **shocked**	泣く naku **cry (v)**	気絶する kizetsu suru **faint (v)**	欠伸する akubi suru **yawn (v)**

人生 jinsei • life events

生まれる
umareru
be born (v)

入学する
nyūgaku suru
start school (v)

友達になる
tomodachi ni naru
make friends (v)

卒業する
sotsugyō suru
graduate (v)

就職する
shūshoku suru
get a job (v)

恋愛する
ren'ai suru
fall in love (v)

結婚する
kekkon suru
get married (v)

出産する
shussan suru
have a baby (v)

結婚式 kekkonshiki | wedding

離婚
rikon
divorce

葬式
sōshiki
funeral

関連用語 kanrenyōgo • vocabulary

洗礼 senrei **christening**	遺言状を書く yuigonjō o kaku **make a will (v)**
記念日 kinembi **anniversary**	出生証明書 shussei shōmeisho **birth certificate**
移民する imin suru **emigrate (v)**	結婚披露宴 kekkon hirōen **wedding reception**
退職する taishoku suru **retire (v)**	ハネムーン hanemūn **honeymoon**
死ぬ shinu **die (v)**	バルミツバー barumitsubā **bar mitzvah**

お祝い oiwai • celebrations

誕生パーティー
tanjō pātī
birthday party

カード
kādo
card

誕生日
tanjōbi
birthday

プレゼント
purezento
present

クリスマス
kurisumasu
Christmas

祭り matsuri • festivals

過越祭
sugikoshimatsuri
Passover

正月
shōgatsu
New Year

カーニバル
kānibaru
carnival

行列
gyōretsu
procession

ラマダーン
ramadān
Ramadan

リボン
ribon
ribbon

感謝祭
kanshasai
Thanksgiving

復活祭
fukkatsusai
Easter

ハロウィーン
harowīn
Halloween

ディワーリ
diwāri
Diwali

外観 gaikan
appearance

子供服 kodomo fuku • children's clothing

赤ちゃん akachan • baby

スノースーツ
sunōsūtsu
snowsuit

肌着
hadagi
bodysuit

ベビーグロー
bebīgurō
onesie

スナップ
sunappu
snap

スリープスーツ
surīpusūtsu
sleeper

ロンパース
rompāsu
romper

よだれ掛け
yodarekake
bib

ミトン
miton
mittens

ブーティ
būti
booties

おむつ
omutsu
terrycloth diaper

紙おむつ
kami omutsu
disposable diaper

おむつカバー
omutsu kabā
plastic pants

幼児 yōji • toddler

Tシャツ
tīshatsu
t-shirt

オーバーオール
ōbāōru
overalls

日よけ帽
hiyokebō
sun hat

半ズボン
hanzubon
shorts

スカート
sukāto
skirt

エプロン
epuron
apron

子供 kodomo · child

ワンピース
wampīsu
dress

フード
fūdo
hood

ジーパン
jīpan
jeans

サンダル
sandaru
sandals

リュックサック
ryukkusakku
backpack

トグルボタン
togurubotan
toggle

マフラー
mafurā
scarf

アノラック
anorakku
parka

長靴
nagagutsu
rain boots

夏
natsu
summer

レインコート
reinkōto
raincoat

秋
aki
fall

ダッフルコート
daffurukōto
duffel coat

冬
fuyu
winter

ナイトガウン
naitogaun
bathrobe

ロゴ
rogo
logo

スニーカー
sunīkā
athletic shoes

ネグリジェ
negurije
nightgown

スリッパ
surippa
slippers

寝間着
nemaki
nightwear

サッカー着
sakkā-gi
soccer uniform

トラックスーツ
torakkusūtsu
running suit

レギンス
reginsu
leggings

関連用語 kanrenyōgo · **vocabulary**

天然繊維
tennen sen'i
natural fiber

合成繊維
gōsei sen'i
synthetic fiber

洗濯機で洗えますか。
sentakki de araemasuka?
Is it machine washable?

2歳児に着れますか。
nisai-ji ni kiremasuka?
Will this fit a two-year-old?

男性服 dansei fuku · men's clothing

襟
eri
collar

ネクタイ
nekutai
tie

ベルト
beruto
belt

ラペル
raperu
lapel

ボタンホール
botanhōru
buttonhole

袖口
sodeguchi
cuff

上着
uwagi
jacket

ズボン
zubon
trousers

ボタン
botan
button

スーツ
sūtsu
business suit

ポケット
poketto
pocket

コート
kōto
coat

裏地
uraji
lining

革靴
kawagutsu
leather
shoes

関連用語 kanrenyōgo · vocabulary

ワイシャツ waishatsu **shirt**	ナイトガウン naitogaun **bathrobe**	トラックスーツ torakkusūtsu **running suit**	長い nagai **long**
カーディガン kādigan **cardigan**	下着 shitagi **underwear**	レインコート reinkōto **raincoat**	短い mijikai **short**

もっと大きい／小さいサイズはありますか。
motto ōki/chīsai saizu wa arimasuka?
Do you have this in a larger/smaller size?

試着できますか。
shichaku dekimasuka?
May I try this on?

Vネック
buinekku
v-neck

丸首
marukubi
round neck

ブレザー
burezā
blazer

スポーツジャケット
supôtsu jaketto
sports jacket

ベスト
besuto
vest

Tシャツ
tīshatsu
t-shirt

アノラック
anorakku
parka

トレーナー
torēnā
sweatshirt

ウインドブレーカー
uindoburēkā
windbreaker

スエットパンツ
suettopantsu
sweatpants

セーター
sētā
sweater

パジャマ
pajama
pajamas

肌着
hadagi
undershirt

カジュアルウェア
kajuaruwea
casual wear

短パン
tampan
shorts

ブリーフ
burīfu
briefs

ボクサーショーツ
bokusāshōtsu
boxer shorts

靴下
kutsushita
socks

女性服 josei fuku • women's clothing

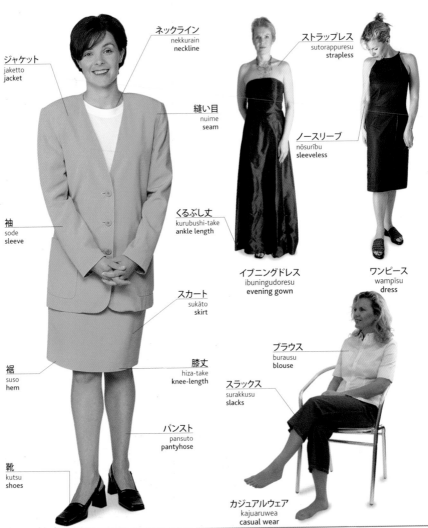

ネックライン
nekkurain
neckline

ジャケット
jaketto
jacket

縫い目
nuime
seam

袖
sode
sleeve

くるぶし丈
kurubushi-take
ankle length

スカート
sukāto
skirt

裾
suso
hem

膝丈
hiza-take
knee-length

パンスト
pansuto
pantyhose

靴
kutsu
shoes

ストラップレス
sutorappuresu
strapless

ノースリーブ
nōsurību
sleeveless

イブニングドレス
ibuningudoresu
evening gown

ワンピース
wampīsu
dress

ブラウス
burausu
blouse

スラックス
surakkusu
slacks

カジュアルウェア
kajuaruwea
casual wear

ランジェリー ranjerī • lingerie

ナイトガウン
naitogaun
negligée

スリップ
surippu
slip

ストラップ
sutorappu
strap

キャミソール
kyamisōru
brra camisole

ガーター
gātā
suspenders

バスク
basuku
bustier

ストッキング
sutokkingu
stockings

パンスト
pansuto
pantyhose

ベスト
besuto
vest

ブラジャー
burajā
bra

パンティ
panti
panties

ネグリジェ
negurije
nightgown

結婚式 kekkonshiki • wedding

ベール
bēru
veil

レース
rēsu
lace

ブーケ
būke
bouquet

トレーン
torēn
train

ウェディングドレス
wedingudoresu
wedding dress

関連用語 kanrenyōgo • vocabulary

コルセット
korusetto
corset

テーラード
tērādo
tailored

ガーター
gātā
garter

ホールターネック
hōrutā nekku
halter neck

ショルダーパッド
shorudāpaddo
shoulder pad

ワイヤーカップ
waiyā kappu
underwired

ウエストバンド
uesutobando
waistband

スポーツ用ブラジャー
supōtsu-yō burajā
sports bra

着物
kimono
kimono

装身具 sōshingu • accessories

バックル
bakkuru
buckle

柄
e
handle

野球帽
yakyūbō
cap

帽子
bōshi
hat

スカーフ
sukāfu
scarf

ベルト
beruto
belt

先端
sentan
tip

ハンカチ
hankachi
handkerchief

蝶ネクタイ
chōnekutai
bow tie

ネクタイピン
nekutaipin
tie clip

手袋
tebukuro
gloves

傘
kasa
umbrella

アクセサリー akusesarī • jewellery

真珠の首飾り
shinju no kubikazari
string of pearls

ペンダント
pendanto
pendant

ブローチ
burōchi
brooch

カフスボタン
kafusubotan
cufflink

リンク
rinku
link

クラスプ
kurasupu
clasp

イヤリング
iyaringu
earring

指輪
yubiwa
ring

宝石
hōseki
stone

ネックレス
nekkuresu
necklace

腕時計
udedokei
watch

ブレスレット
buresuretto
bracelet

チェーン
chēn
chain

宝石箱 hōseki-bako | jewelry box

バッグ baggu • bags

札入れ
satsuire
wallet

財布
saifu
change purse

ショルダーバッグ
shorudābaggu
shoulder bag

留め金
tomegane
fastening

ストラップ
sutorappu
shoulder strap

取っ手
totte
handles

旅行鞄
ryokōkaban
duffle bag

ブリーフケース
burīfukēsu
briefcase

ハンドバッグ
handobaggu
handbag

リュックサック
ryukkusakku
backpack

靴 kutsu • shoes

靴紐穴
kutsuhimo ana
eyelet

靴紐
kutsuhimo
lace

ベロ
bero
tongue

靴底
kutsuzoko
sole

踵
kakato
heel

編上靴
amiagegutsu
lace-up

ハイキングブーツ
haikingu būtsu
hiking boot

スニーカー
sunīkā
athletic shoe

革靴
kawagutsu
leather shoe

ゴム草履
gomuzōri
flip-flop

ハイヒール
haihīru
high-heeled shoe

プラットフォームシューズ
purattofōmu shūzu
platform shoe

サンダル
sandaru
sandal

スリッポン
surippon
slip-on

短靴
tangutsu
wingtip

髪 kami • hair

櫛
kushi
comb

櫛で梳く
kushi de suku
comb (v)

ヘアブラシ
heaburashi
brush

ブラシをかける
burashi o kakeru | brush (v)

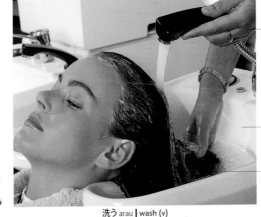

髪結い
kamiyui
hairdresser

シャンプー台
shampū dai
sink

客
kyaku
client

洗う arau | wash (v)

濯ぐ
yusugu
rinse (v)

カットする
katto suru
cut (v)

ガウン
gaun
cape

ブローする
burō suru
blow dry (v)

セットする
setto suru
set (v)

備品 bihin • accessories

ヘアドライヤー
headoraiyā
hairdryer

シャンプー
shampū
shampoo

コンディショナー
kondishonā
conditioner

ジェル
jeru
gel

ヘアスプレー
heasupurē
hairspray

カールアイロン
kāru airon
curling iron

鋏
hasami
scissors

ヘアバンド
heabando
headband

カーラー
kārā
curler

ヘアピン
heapin
bobby pin

髪型 kamigata • styles

リボン
ribon
ribbon

ポニーテール
ponītēru
ponytail

三つ編み
mitsuami
braid

フレンチプリーツ
furenchi purītsu
french twist

お団子
odango
bun

お下げ
osage
pigtails

ボブ
bobu
bob

坊ちゃん刈り
botchangari
crop

カール
kāru
curly

パーマ
pāma
perm

ストレート
sutorēto
straight

毛根
mōkon
roots

ハイライト
hairaito
highlights

はげ頭
hageatama
bald

鬘
katsura
wig

関連用語 kanrenyōgo • vocabulary

整髪する
seihatsu suru
trim (v)

脂質
abura shitsu
greasy

ストレートにする
sutorēto ni suru
straighten (v)

乾燥質
kansō shitsu
dry

床屋
tokoya
barber

普通
futsū
normal

フケ
fuke
dandruff

頭皮
tōhi
scalp

枝毛
edage
split ends

ヘアタイ
heatai
hair tie

ヘアカラー hea karā • colors

ブロンド
burondo
blonde

ブルネット
burunetto
brunette

赤茶色
akachairo
auburn

赤毛
akage
ginger

黒髪
kurokami
black

グレー
gurē
gray

ホワイト
howaito
white

染髪
sempatsu
dyed

美容 biyō • beauty

ヘアカラー
heakarā
hair dye

アイシャドー
aishadō
eye shadow

マスカラ
masukara
mascara

アイライナー
airainā
eyeliner

頬紅
hōbeni
blusher

ファンデーション
fandêshon
foundation

口紅
kuchibeni
lipstick

メーキャップ mēkyappu • makeup

アイブロウペンシル
aiburow penshiru
eyebrow pencil

アイブロウブラシ
aiburow burashi
eyebrow brush

毛抜き
kenuki
tweezers

リップグロス
rippu gurosu
lip gloss

リップブラシ
rippu burashi
lip brush

リップライナー
rippu rainā
lip liner

ブラシ
burashi
brush

コンシーラー
konshīrā
concealer

コンパクトミラー
kompakuto mirā
mirror

白粉
oshiroi
face powder

パフ
pafu
powder puff

コンパクト kompakuto | compact

エステ esute • beauty treatments

フェースパック
fēsu pakku
facial mask

サンベッド
sambeddo
sunbed

角質除去する
kakushitsu jokyo suru
exfoliate (v)

フェーシャル
fēsharu
facial

ワックス
wakkusu
wax

ペディキュア
pedikyua
pedicure

化粧品 keshōhin • toiletries

クレンザー
kurenzā
cleanser

化粧水
keshōsui
toner

乳液
nyūeki
moisturizer

セルフタンニング・クリーム
serufu tanningu kurīmu
self-tanning cream

香水
kōsui
perfume

オードトワレ
ōdotoware
eau de toilette

マニキュア manikyua • manicure

除光液
jokō eki
nail varnish remover

爪やすり
tsume yasuri
nail file

マニキュア
manikyua
nail varnish

爪切り鋏
tsumekiri-basami
nail scissors

爪切り
tsumekiri
nail clippers

関連用語 kanrenyōgo • vocabulary

肌の色 hada no iro **complexion**	脂肌 abura hada **oily**	日焼け hiyake **tan**
色白 irojiro **fair**	敏感肌 binkan hada **sensitive**	入れ墨 irezumi **tattoo**
色黒 iroguro **dark**	低刺激性 tei-shigeki sei **hypoallergenic**	皺取り shiwa tori **anti-wrinkle**
乾燥肌 kansō hada **dry**	色合い iroai **shade**	コットンボール kotton bōru **cotton balls**

健康 kenkō
health

病気 byōki • illness

熱 netsu | fever

頭痛
zutsū
headache

鼻血
hanaji
nosebleed

咳
seki
cough

くしゃみ
kushami
sneeze

風邪
kaze
cold

インフルエンザ
infuruenza
flu

吸入器
kyūnyūki
inhaler

喘息
zensoku
asthma

腹痛
fukutsū
cramps

吐き気
hakike
nausea

水痘
suitō
chickenpox

発疹
hosshin
rash

関連用語 kanrenyōgo • vocabulary

脳卒中 nōsotchū **stroke**	糖尿病 tōnyōbyō **diabetes**	アトピー性皮膚炎 atopīsei hifuen **eczema**	悪寒 okan **chill**	吐く haku **vomit (v)**	下痢 geri **diarrhea**
血圧 ketsuatsu **blood pressure**	アレルギー arerugī **allergy**	感染 kansen **infection**	胃痛 itsū **stomach ache**	癲癇 tenkan **epilepsy**	麻疹 hashika **measles**
心臓発作 shinzōhossa **heart attack**	花粉症 kafunshō **hayfever**	ウイルス uirusu **virus**	失神する shisshin suru **faint (v)**	片頭痛 henzutsū **migraine**	おたふく風邪 otafukukaze **mumps**

医者 isha • doctor
診察 shinsatsu • consultation

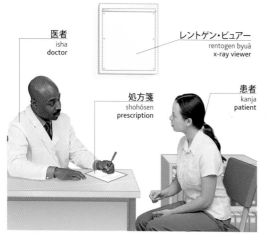

医者
isha
doctor

レントゲン・ビュアー
rentogen byuā
x-ray viewer

処方箋
shohōsen
prescription

患者
kanja
patient

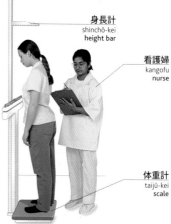

身長計
shinchō-kei
height bar

看護婦
kangofu
nurse

体重計
taijū-kei
scale

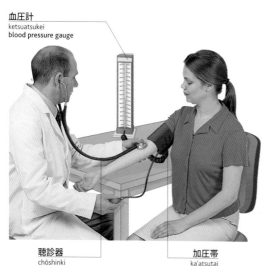

血圧計
ketsuatsukei
blood pressure gauge

聴診器
chōshinki
stethoscope

加圧帯
ka'atsutai
cuff

関連用語 kanrenyōgo • vocabulary

予約
yoyaku
appointment

予防接種
yobō-sesshu
inoculation

診療室
shinryō-shitsu
doctor's office

体温計
taionkei
thermometer

待合室
machiai-shitsu
waiting room

診察
shinsatsu
medical examination

医者に行かなければなりません。
isha ni ikanakereba narimasen.
I need to see a doctor.

ここが痛い。
koko ga itai.
It hurts here.

怪我 kega • injury

捌挫 nenza | sprain

三角布
sankakufu
sling

骨折
kossetsu
fracture

ギブス
gibusu
neck brace

鞭打ち症
muchiuchishō
whiplash

切り傷
kirikizu
cut

擦り傷
surikizu
abrasion

痣
aza
bruise

刺
toge
splinter

日焼け
hiyake
sunburn

火傷
yakedo
burn

かみ傷
kamikizu
bite

虫刺され
mushi-sasare
sting

関連用語 kanrenyōgo • vocabulary

事故 jiko accident	出血 shukketsu hemorrhage	中毒 chūdoku poisoning	大丈夫でしょうか。 daijōbu deshōka? Will he/she be all right?
緊急事態 kinkyūjitai emergency	水ぶくれ mizubukure blister	感電 kanden electric shock	どこが痛みますか。 doko ga itamimasuka? Where does it hurt?
傷 kizu wound	脳しんとう nōshintō concussion	頭部外傷 tōbu gaishō head injury	救急車を呼んでください。 kyūkyūsha o yonde kudasai. Please call an ambulance.

応急手当 ōkyū teate • first aid

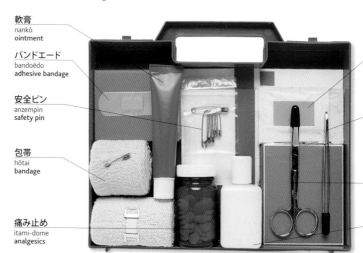

軟膏
nankō
ointment

バンドエード
bandoēdo
adhesive bandage

安全ピン
anzempin
safety pin

包帯
hōtai
bandage

痛み止め
itami-dome
analgesics

消毒ワイプ
shōdoku waipu
antiseptic wipe

ピンセット
pinsetto
tweezers

鋏
hasami
scissors

消毒液
shōdoku eki
antiseptic

救急箱 kyūkyūbako | first aid box

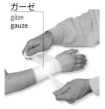

ガーゼ
gāze
gauze

手当
teate
dressing

副木 fukuboku | splint

絆創膏
bansōkō
adhesive tape

救急蘇生
kyūkyū sosei
resuscitation

関連用語 kanrenyōgo • vocabulary

ショック shokku **shock**	脈拍 myakuhaku **pulse**	窒息する chissoku suru **choke (v)**	助けてください。 tasukete kudasai. **Please help.**
意識不明 ishikifumei **unconscious**	呼吸 kokyū **breathing**	殺菌 sakkin **sterile**	応急手当のやり方を知っていますか。 ōkyū teate no yarikata o shitte imasuka? **Do you know first aid?**

病院 byōin • hospital

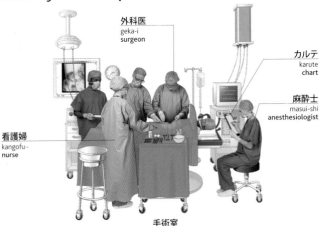

外科医
geka-i
surgeon

看護婦
kangofu~
nurse

手術室
shujutsu-shitsu
operating room

カルテ
karute
chart

麻酔士
masui-shi
anesthesiologist

血液検査
ketsueki kensa
blood test

注射
chūsha
injection

レントゲン
rentogen
x-ray

スキャン
sukyan
scan

車輪付き担架
sharin-tsuki tanka
gurney

緊急治療室
kinkyū chiryō-shitsu
emergency room

呼び出しボタン
yobidashi botan
call button

病室
byōshitsu
hospital room

車椅子
kurumaisu
wheelchair

関連用語 kanrenyōgo • vocabulary

手術 shujutsu operation	退院 tai'in discharged	面会時間 menkai jikan visiting hours	小児病棟 shōni byōtō children's ward	集中治療室 shūchū chiryō-shitsu intensive care unit
入院 nyūin admitted	診療所 shinryōjo clinic	産科病棟 sanka byōtō maternity ward	個室 koshitsu private room	外来患者 gairaikanja outpatient

医療部門 iryō bumon · departments

耳鼻咽喉科
jibi'inkō-ka
ears, nose, and throat (ENT)

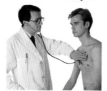
心臓病科
shinzōbyō-ka
cardiology

整形外科
seikeige-ka
orthopedics

婦人科
fujin-ka
gynecology

理学療法科
rigakuryōhō-ka
physical therapy

皮膚科
hifu-ka
dermatology

小児科
shōni-ka
pediatrics

放射線科
hōshasen-ka
radiology

外科
geka
surgery

産科
sanka
maternity

精神科
seishin-ka
psychiatry

眼科
ganka
ophthalmology

関連用語 kanrenyōgo · vocabulary

神経科
shinkei-ka
neurology

泌尿器科
hinyōki-ka
urology

内分泌科
naibumpi-ka
endocrinology

病理科
byōri-ka
pathology

結果
kekka
result

癌科
gan-ka
oncology

形成外科
keisei-geka
plastic surgery

照会
shōkai
referral

検査
kensa
test

専門医
senmon'i
specialist

歯医者 haisha • dentist

歯 ha • tooth

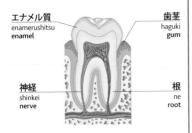

エナメル質
enamerushitsu
enamel

歯茎
haguki
gum

神経
shinkei
nerve

根
ne
root

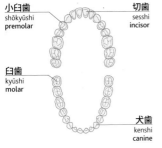

小臼歯
shōkyūshi
premolar

切歯
sesshi
incisor

臼歯
kyūshi
molar

犬歯
kenshi
canine

関連用語 kanrenyōgo • vocabulary

歯痛 haita toothache	ドリル doriru drill
歯垢 shikō plaque	デンタルフロス dentaru furosu dental floss
虫歯 mushiba decay	抜歯 basshi extraction
詰め物 tsumemono filling	歯冠 shikan crown

歯科検診 shika kenshin • checkup

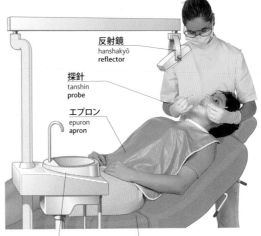

反射鏡
hanshakyō
reflector

探針
tanshin
probe

エプロン
epuron
apron

うがい台
ugai dai
basin

歯科ユニット
shika yunitto
dentist's chair

デンタルフロスで掃除する
dentaru furosu de sōji suru
floss (v)

歯磨きする
hamigaki suru
brush (v)

歯列矯正ブリッジ
shiretsu kyōsei burijji
braces

歯科レントゲン
shika rentogen
dental x-ray

レントゲン写真
rentogen shashin
x-ray film

入れ歯
ireba
dentures

眼鏡店 megane-ten • optician

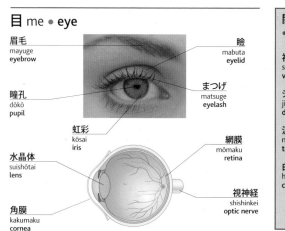

ケース
kēsu
case

レンズ
renzu
lens

フレーム
furēmu
frame

眼鏡
megane
glasses

サングラス
sangurasu
sunglasses

洗浄液
senjō eki
cleaning fluid

消毒液
shōdoku eki
disinfectant solution

レンズケース
renzu kēsu
lens case

視力検査 shiryoku kensa | **eye test**

コンタクトレンズ kontakutorenzu | **contact lenses**

目 me • eye

眉毛
mayuge
eyebrow

瞼
mabuta
eyelid

瞳孔
dōkō
pupil

まつげ
matsuge
eyelash

虹彩
kōsai
iris

網膜
mōmaku
retina

水晶体
suishōtai
lens

視神経
shishinkei
optic nerve

角膜
kakumaku
cornea

関連用語 kanrenyōgo • vocabulary

視力
shiryoku
vision

乱視
ranshi
astigmatism

ジオプター
jioputā
diopter

遠視
enshi
farsightedness

涙
namida
tear

近視
kinshi
nearsightedness

白内障
hakunaishō
cataract

遠近両用
enkin ryōyō
bifocal

妊娠 ninshin · **pregnancy**

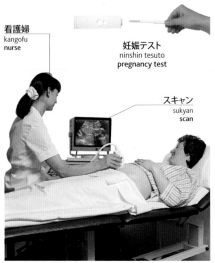

看護婦
kangofu
nurse

妊娠テスト
ninshin tesuto
pregnancy test

スキャン
sukyan
scan

超音波（検査）chōompa (kensa) | ultrasound (test)

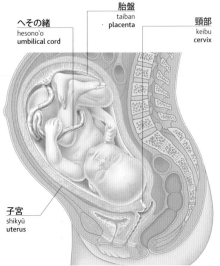

胎盤
taiban
placenta

へその緒
hesono'o
umbilical cord

頸部
keibu
cervix

子宮
shikyū
uterus

胎児 taiji | fetus

関連用語 kanrenyōgo · vocabulary

排卵 hairan **ovulation**	**出産前** shussan mae **prenatal**	**陣痛** jintsū **contraction**	**子宮頸部拡張** shikyū keibu kakuchō **dilation**	**分娩** bumben **delivery**	**逆子** sakago **breech**
受胎 jutai **conception**	**胚** hai **embryo**	**破水する** hasui suru **break waters (v)**	**硬膜外麻酔** kōmaku-gai masui **epidural**	**誕生** tanjō **birth**	**未熟児** mijukuji **premature**
妊娠 ninshin **pregnant**	**子宮** shikyū **uterus**	**羊水** yōsui **amniotic fluid**	**会陰切開** kai'in sekkai **episiotomy**	**流産** ryūzan **miscarriage**	**婦人科医** fujinka-i **gynecologist**
妊娠している ninshin shiteiru **expectant**	**三半期** sanhanki **trimester**	**羊水穿刺** yōsui senshi **amniocentesis**	**帝王切開** teiō sekkai **cesarean section**	**縫合** hōgō **stitches**	**産科医** sanka-i **obstetrician**

出産 shussan • childbirth

点滴
tenteki
drip

助産婦
josampu
midwife

モニター
monitā
monitor

カテーテル
katēteru
catheter

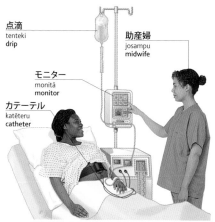

陣痛促進する jintsū sokushin suru | induce labor (v)

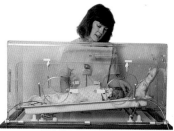

保育器 hoikuki | incubator

赤ちゃん用体重計
akachan-yō taijūkei
scale

出生時体重 shussei-ji taijū | birth weight

鉗子
kanshi
forceps

真空カップ
shinkū kappu
suction cup

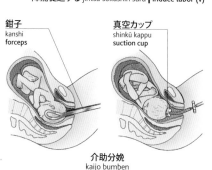

介助分娩
kaijo bumben
assisted delivery

識別バンド
shikibetsu bando
identification tag

新生児 shinseiji | newborn baby

授乳 junyū • nursing

搾乳機
sakunyū-ki
breast pump

授乳ブラジャー
junyū burajā
nursing bra

授乳する
junyū suru
breastfeed (v)

パッド
paddo
pads

代替療法 daitai ryōhō • **alternative therapy**

先生
sensei
teacher

マッサージ
massāji
massage

指圧
shiatsu
shiatsu

ヨガ yoga | **yoga**

マット
matto
mat

瞑想
meisō
meditation

カイロプラクティック
kairopurakutikku
chiropractic

整骨療法
seikotsu ryōhō
osteopathy

リフレクソロジー
rifurekusorojī
reflexology

カウンセラー
kaunserā
counselor

グループ療法
gurūpu ryōhō
group therapy

レイキ療法
reiki ryōhō
reiki

アユルヴェーダ
ayuruvēda
ayurveda

鍼療法
hari ryōhō
acupuncture

催眠療法
saimin ryōhō
hypnotherapy

精油
seiyu
essential oils

本草学
honsō-gaku
herbalism

アロマテラピー
aromaterapī
aromatherapy

ホメオパシー
homeopashī
homeopathy

指圧療法
shiatsu ryōhō
acupressure therapy

療法士
ryōhōshi
therapist

心理療法
shinri ryōhō
psychotherapy

関連用語 kanrenyōgo • **vocabulary**			
サプリメント sapurimento **supplement**	自然療法 shizen ryōhō **naturopathy**	リラクセーション rirakusēshon **relaxation**	薬草 yakusō **herb**
水治療法 suichi ryōhō **hydrotherapy**	風水 fūsui **feng shui**	ストレス sutoresu **stress**	水晶療法 suishō ryōhō **crystal healing**

家庭 katei
home

住宅 jūtaku • house

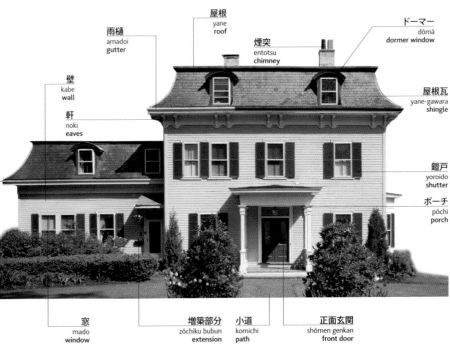

屋根
yane
roof

雨樋
amadoi
gutter

ドーマー
dōmā
dormer window

煙突
entotsu
chimney

壁
kabe
wall

屋根瓦
yane-gawara
shingle

軒
noki
eaves

鎧戸
yoroido
shutter

ポーチ
pōchi
porch

窓
mado
window

増築部分
zōchiku bubun
extension

小道
komichi
path

正面玄関
shōmen genkan
front door

関連用語 kanrenyōgo • vocabulary

一戸建て ikkodate **detached**	借家人 shakuyanin **tenant**	車庫 shako **garage**	郵便受け yūbin-uke **letter slot**	防犯ベル bōhan beru **burglar alarm**	貸す kasu **rent (v)**
セミデタッチ semidetatchi **semidetached**	平屋 hiraya **bungalow**	屋根裏部屋 yaneura-beya **attic**	玄関灯 genkan-tō **porch light**	中庭 nakaniwa **courtyard**	家賃 yachin **rent**
タウンハウス taunhausu **townhouse**	地下室 chikashitsu **basement**	部屋 heya **room**	大家 ōya **landlord**	床 yuka **floor**	テラス terasu **terraced**

入口 iriguchi • entrance

手摺
tesuri
hand rail

踊り場
odoriba
landing

階段の手摺
kaidan no tesuri
banister

階段
kaidan
staircase

玄関
genkan
hallway

呼び鈴
yobirin
doorbell

玄関マット
genkan matto
doormat

ドアノッカー
doanokkā
door knocker

ドアチェーン
doachēn
door chain

鍵
kagi
key

錠
jō
lock

閂
kannuki
bolt

マンション manshon • apartment

ベランダ
beranda
balcony

マンション棟
manshon-tō
apartment building

インターホン
intāhon
intercom

エレベーター
erebētā
elevator

住宅内設備 jūtaku-nai setsubi • **utilities**

羽
hane
blade

扇風機
sempūki
fan

ラジエーター
rajiētā
radiator

ヒーター
hītā
space heater

ファンヒーター
fanhītā
portable heater

電気設備 denki setsubi • **electricity**

フィラメント
firamento
filament

接地ピン
setchi pin
ground prong

バヨネット式
bayonetto-shiki
thread

ピン
pin
prong

マイナス
mainasu
neutral

プラス
purasu
live

電球 denkyū | **light bulb**

プラグ puragu | **plug**

電線 densen | **wires**

関連用語 kanrenyōgo • **vocabulary**

電圧 den'atsu **voltage**	ヒューズ hyūzu **fuse**	コンセント konsento **outlet**	直流電流 chokuryū denryū **direct current (DC)**	停電 teiden **power outage**
アンペア ampea **amp**	ヒューズボックス hyūzu bokkusu **fuse box**	スイッチ suitchi **switch**	変圧器 hen'atsuki **transformer**	電源 dengen **domestic supply**
電力 denryoku **power**	発電機 hatsudenki **generator**	交流電流 kōryū denryū **alternating current (AC)**	電力量計 denryokuryō-kei **electricity meter**	

配管設備 haikan setsubi • **plumbing**

流し台 nagashidai • **sink**

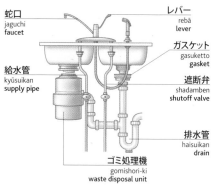

蛇口
jaguchi
faucet

レバー
rebā
lever

ガスケット
gasuketto
gasket

給水管
kyūsuikan
supply pipe

遮断弁
shadamben
shutoff valve

排水管
haisuikan
drain

ゴミ処理機
gomishori-ki
waste disposal unit

オーバーフロー管
ōbāfurō kan
overflow pipe

吸水口
kyūsui-kō
inlet

出水口
shussui-kō
outlet

圧力バルブ
atsuryoku
barubu
**pressure
valve**

保温材
ho'onzai
insulation

温水タンク
onsui tanku
tank

水室
suishitsu
**water
chamber**

排水コック
haisuikokku
drain cock

サーモスタット
sāmosutatto
thermostat

ガスバーナー
gasubānā
gas burner

ボイラー
boirā
water heater

発熱体
hatsunetsutai
heating element

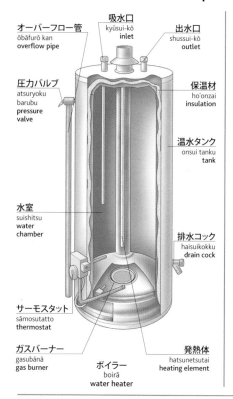

トイレ toire • **toilet**

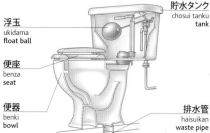

貯水タンク
chosui tanku
tank

浮玉
ukidama
float ball

便座
benza
seat

便器
benki
bowl

排水管
haisuikan
waste pipe

ゴミ処理 gomishori • **waste disposal**

ボトル
botoru
bottle

ペダル
pedaru
pedal

リサイクルボックス
risaikuru bokkusu
recycling bin

蓋
futa
lid

ゴミ箱
gomibako
trash can

分別ユニット
bumbetsu yunitto
sorting unit

有機ゴミ
yūki gomi
organic waste

居間 ima • living room

絵
e
painting

額縁
gakubuchi
frame

ランプ
rampu
lamp

壁面照明
hekimen shōmei
wall light

時計
tokei
clock

天井
tenjō
ceiling

食器棚
shokkidana
cabinet

ソファ
sofa
sofa

クッション
kusshon
cushion

コーヒーテーブル
kōhī tēburu
coffee table

床
yuka
floor

日本語 nihongo • english

鏡
kagami
mirror

花瓶
kabin
vase

マントルピース
mantorupīsu
mantlepiece

暖炉
danro
fireplace

ファイヤースクリーン
faiyā sukurīn
screen

蝋燭
rōsoku
candle

本棚
hondana
bookshelf

ソファベッド
sofa beddo
sofabed

絨毯
jūtan
rug

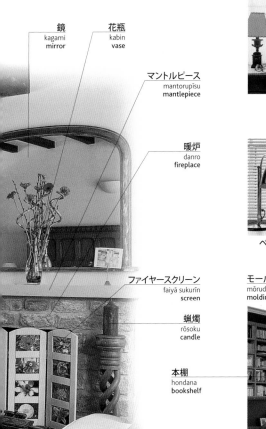

カーテン
kāten
curtain

メッシュカーテン
messhu kāten
sheer curtain

ベネシャンブラインド
beneshan buraindo
venetian blind

ロールスクリーン
rōru sukurīn
window shade

モールディング
mōrudingu
molding

アームチェア
āmuchea
armchair

書斎 shosai | **study**

ダイニングルーム daningu rūmu • **dining room**

胡椒
koshō
pepper

塩
shio
salt

テーブル
tēburu
table

食器
shokki
dishes

椅子
isu
chair

背もたれ
semotare
back

座面
zamen
seat

脚
ashi
leg

関連用語 kanrenyōgo • **vocabulary**

給仕する kyūji suru **serve (v)**	朝食 chōshoku **breakfast**	満腹 mampuku **full**	箸 hashi **chopsticks**	おかわりできますか。 okawari dekimasuka? **May I have some more, please?**
食べる taberu **eat (v)**	昼食 chūshoku **lunch**	一人分 hitoribun **one portion**	ご飯茶碗 gohan-jawan **rice bowl**	もう結構です。 mō kekkō desu. **I've had enough, thank you.**
空腹 kūfuku **hungry**	夕食 yūshoku **dinner**	食事 shokuji **meal**	茶碗 chawan **(Japanese) teacup**	美味しかったです。 oishikatta desu. **That was delicious.**
テーブルクロス tēburukurosu **tablecloth**	ランチョンマット ranchon matto **placemat**	客 kyaku **guest**	座布団 zabuton **(Japanese) floor cushion**	

食器類 shokki rui • dishes and utensils

マグカップ
magu kappu
mug

コーヒーカップ
kōhīkappu
coffee cup

ティーカップ
tīkappu
teacup

ティースプーン
tīsupūn
teaspoon

皿
sara
plate

ボウル
bōru
bowl

カフェプレス
kafe puresu
cafetière

ティーポット
tīpotto
teapot

水差し
mizusashi
pitcher

エッグカップ
eggu kappu
egg cup

ワイングラス
waingurasu
wine glass

タンブラー
tamburā
tumbler

コップ類
koppu rui
glassware

ナプキンリング
napukin ringu
napkin ring

小皿
kozara
side plate

大皿
ōzara
dinner plate

スープ皿
sūpuzara
soup bowl

スープスプーン
sūpusupūn
soup spoon

ナプキン
napukin
napkin

フォーク
fōku
fork

テーブル・セッティング
tēburu settingu
place setting

スプーン
supūn
spoon

ナイフ
naifu
knife

台所 daidokoro • **kitchen**

換気扇
kankisen
extractor fan

棚
tana
shelves

水はね防止板
mizuhane bōshi-ban
splashback

セラミックコンロ
seramikku konro
ceramic stovetop

蛇口
jaguchi
faucet

調理台
chōridai
countertop

流し
nagashi
sink

オーブン
ōbun
oven

引き出し
hikidashi
drawer

戸棚
todana
cabinet

電気器具 denki kigu • **appliances**

電子レンジ
denshirenji
microwave oven

ミキシングボウル
mikishingubōru
mixing bowl

蓋
futa
lid

ブレード
burēdo
blade

電気やかん
denki yakan
electric kettle

トースター
tōsutā
toaster

フードプロセッサー
fūdopurosessā
food processor

ミキサー
mikisā
blender

皿洗い機
sara'arai-ki
dishwasher

日本語 nihongo • **english**

製氷室
seihyōshitsu
icemaker

冷蔵庫
reizōko
refrigerator

棚
tana
shelf

冷凍庫
reitōko
freezer

野菜室
yasai-shitsu
crisper

冷凍冷蔵庫 reitōreizōko |refrigerator-freezer

関連用語 kanrenyōgo
• vocabulary

水切り台
mizukiridai
drainboard

冷凍する
reitō suru
freeze (v)

ガスレンジ
gasurenji
burner

解凍する
kaitō suru
defrost (v)

コンロ
konro
stovetop

蒸す
musu
steam (v)

ゴミ箱
gomibako
garbage can

炒める
itameru
sauté (v)

調理 chōri • cooking

皮を剥く
kawa o muku
peel (v)

切る
kiru
slice (v)

すり下ろす
suriorosu
grate (v)

注ぐ
sosogu
pour (v)

混ぜる
mazeru
mix (v)

泡立てる
awadateru
whisk (v)

茹でる
yuderu
boil (v)

揚げる
ageru
fry (v)

巻く
maku
roll (v)

かき回す
kakimawasu
stir (v)

煮込む
nikomu
simmer (v)

（沸騰前の温度で）茹でる
(futtō mae no ondo de) yuderu
poach (v)

（オーブンで）焼く
(ōbun de) yaku
bake (v)

ローストする
rōsuto suru
roast (v)

焼く
yaku
grill (v)

調理用具 chōri yōgu • kitchenware

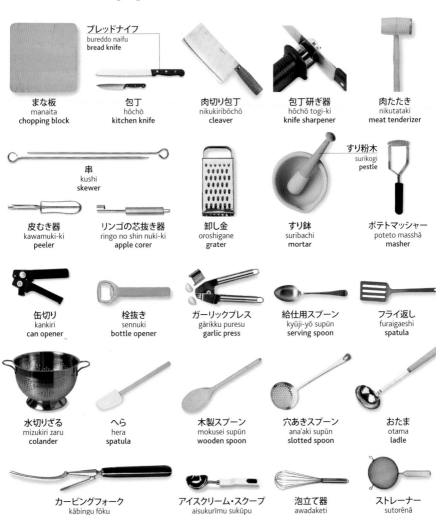

ブレッドナイフ
bureddo naifu
bread knife

まな板
manaita
chopping block

包丁
hōchō
kitchen knife

肉切り包丁
nikukiribōchō
cleaver

包丁研ぎ器
hōchō togi-ki
knife sharpener

肉たたき
nikutataki
meat tenderizer

串
kushi
skewer

すり粉木
surikogi
pestle

皮むき器
kawamuki-ki
peeler

リンゴの芯抜き器
ringo no shin nuki-ki
apple corer

卸し金
oroshigane
grater

すり鉢
suribachi
mortar

ポテトマッシャー
poteto masshā
masher

缶切り
kankiri
can opener

栓抜き
sennuki
bottle opener

ガーリックプレス
gārikku puresu
garlic press

給仕用スプーン
kyūji-yō supūn
serving spoon

フライ返し
furaigaeshi
spatula

水切りざる
mizukiri zaru
colander

へら
hera
spatula

木製スプーン
mokusei supūn
wooden spoon

穴あきスプーン
ana'aki supūn
slotted spoon

おたま
otama
ladle

カービングフォーク
kābingu fōku
carving fork

アイスクリーム・スクープ
aisukurīmu sukūpu
scoop

泡立て器
awadateki
whisk

ストレーナー
sutorēnā
strainer

蓋
futa
lid

テフロン加工
tefuron kakō
nonstick

フライパン
furaipan
skillet

片手鍋
katate nabe
saucepan

グリルパン
gurirupan
grill pan

中華鍋
chūka nabe
wok

土鍋
donabe
earthenware dish

ガラス製
garasusei
glass

耐熱性
tainetsusei
ovenproof

ミキシングボウル
mikishingu bōru
mixing bowl

ココット
kokotto
soufflé dish

グラタン皿
guratan-zara
gratin dish

ラミキン
ramikin
ramekin

キャセロール鍋
kyaserōru nabe
casserole dish

ケーキ作り kēki-zukuri • baking cakes

秤
hakari
scale

計量ジャグ
keiryō jagu
measuring cup

ケーキ焼き型
kēki yaki-gata
cake tin

パイ焼き皿
pai yaki-zara
pie tin

タルト型
taruto-gata
flan tin

刷毛 hake
pastry brush

のし棒 noshibō
rolling pin

絞り袋 shibori bukuro
piping bag

マフィン型
mafin-gata
muffin tray

ベーキングトレイ
bēkingu torei
baking tray

クーリングラック
kūringu rakku
cooling rack

オーブンミット
ōbunmitto
oven mitt

エプロン
epuron
apron

寝室 shinshitsu • **bedroom**

洋服ダンス
yōfukudansu
wardrobe

ベッドサイドランプ
beddosaido rampu
bedside lamp

ヘッドボード
heddobōdo
headboard

ベッドサイドテーブル
beddosaido tēburu
bedside table

タンス
tansu
chest of drawers

引き出し
hikidashi
drawer

ベッド
beddo
bed

マットレス
mattoresu
mattress

ベッドカバー
beddokabā
bedspread

枕
makura
pillow

湯たんぽ
yutampo
hot-water bottle

時計付きラジオ
tokei-tsuki rajio
clock radio

目覚まし時計
mezamashi-dokei
alarm clock

ティッシュの箱
tisshu no hako
box of tissues

ハンガー
hangâ
coat hanger

ベッド beddo • bed

鏡
kagami
mirror

化粧台
keshōdai
dressing table

床
yuka
floor

枕カバー
makurakabā
pillowcase

シーツ
shītsu
sheet

ベッドスカート
beddo sukāto
dust ruffle

羽布団
hanebuton
comforter

キルト
kiruto
quilt

毛布
mōfu
blanket

関連用語 kanrenyōgo • vocabulary

シングルベッド shinguru beddo **twin bed**	フットボード futtobōdo **footboard**	不眠症 fuminshō **insomnia**	目覚める mezameru **wake up (v)**	目覚ましをかける mezamashi o kakeru **set the alarm (v)**
ダブルベッド daburu beddo **full bed**	スプリング supuringu **spring**	床につく toko ni tsuku **go to bed (v)**	起きる okiru **get up (v)**	鼾をかく ibiki o kaku **snore (v)**
布団 futon **comforter**	カーペット kāpetto **carpet**	寝る neru **go to sleep (v)**	ベッドメーキングする beddomēkingu suru **make the bed (v)**	電気毛布 denkimōfu **electric blanket**

浴室 yokushitsu • bathroom

タオル掛け
taorukake
towel rack

シャワードア
shawā doa
shower door

冷水タップ
reisui tappu
cold faucet

温水タップ
onsui tappu
hot faucet

シャワーヘッド
shawāheddo
shower head

流し台
nagashidai
sink

栓
sen
plug

シャワー
shawā
showerstall

排水口
haisuikō
drain

便座
benza
toilet seat

便器
benki
toilet

トイレブラシ
toire burashi
toilet brush

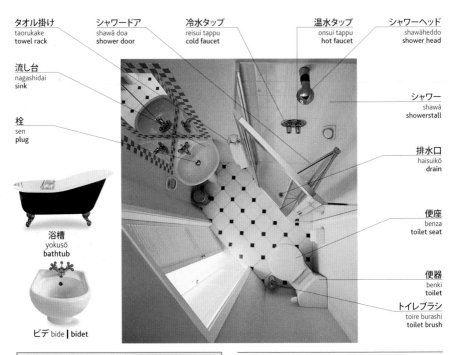

浴槽
yokusō
bathtub

ビデ bide | **bidet**

関連用語 kanrenyōgo • **vocabulary**

浴室用キャビネット
yokushitsu-yō kyabinetto
medicine cabinet

バスマット
basu matto
bath mat

トイレットペーパー
toiretto pēpā
toilet paper

シャワーカーテン
shawā kāten
shower curtain

シャワーを浴びる
shawā o abiru
take a shower (v)

風呂に入る
furo ni hairu
take a bath (v)

歯の手入れ ha no teire • **dental hygiene**

歯ブラシ
haburashi
toothbrush

デンタルフロス
dentaru furosu
dental floss

歯磨き粉
hamigakiko
toothpaste

マウスウォッシュ
mausu wosshu
mouthwash

ヘチマ
hechima
loofah

スポンジ
suponji
sponge

軽石
karuishi
pumice stone

背中洗いブラシ
senaka arai burashi
back brush

デオドラント
deodoranto
deodorant

石鹸皿
sekken-zara
soap dish

シャワージェル
shawā jeru
shower gel

石鹸
sekken
soap

フェースクリーム
fēsu kurīmu
face cream

バブルバス
baburu basu
bubble bath

ハンドタオル
hando taoru
hand towel

バスタオル
basu taoru
bath towel

タオル
taoru
towels

ボディローション
bodi rōshon
body lotion

タルカムパウダー
tarukamu paudā
talcum powder

バスローブ
basurōbu
bathrobe

髭剃り higesori • **shaving**

電気剃刀
denki kamisori
electric razor

髭剃りクリーム
higesori kurīmu
shaving cream

カミソリの刃
kamisori no ha
razor blade

使い捨てカミソリ
tsukaisute kamisori
disposable razor

アフターシェーブ
afutāshēbu
aftershave

子供部屋 kodomobeya・nursery

ベビーケア bebī kea・baby care

スポンジ
suponji
sponge

オムツかぶれクリーム
omutsu kabure kurīmu
diaper rash cream

おしり拭き
oshiri fuki
wet wipe

ベビーバス
bebī basu
baby bath

おまる
omaru
potty

おむつ替えシート
omutsu kae shīto
changing mat

睡眠 suimin・sleeping

モビール
mobīru
mobile

シーツ
shītsu
sheet

毛布
mōfu
blanket

柵
saku
bars

フリース
furīsu
fleece

ベッドバンパー
beddo bampā
bumper

寝具
shingu
bedding

マットレス
mattoresu
mattress

ベビーベッド bebībeddo | crib

ガラガラ
garagara
rattle

新生児用かご型ベッド
shinseiji-yō kago-gata beddo
bassinet

遊び asobi・playing

人形
ningyō
doll

縫いぐるみ
nuigurumi
soft toy

ドールハウス
dōru hausu
dollhouse

子供の家
kodomo no ie
playhouse

テディベア
tedibea
teddy bear

おもちゃ
omocha
toy

おもちゃ籠
omocha kago
toy basket

ボール
bōru
ball

ベビーサークル
bebīsākuru
playpen

安全用品
anzen yōhin
・safety

戸棚ロック
todana rokku
child lock

ベビーモニター
bebī monitā
baby monitor

ベビーゲート
bebī gēto
stair gate

食事 shokuji
・eating

ハイチェア
haichea
high chair

乳首
chikubi
nipple

ベビー用マグカップ
bebī-yō magu kappu
drinking cup

哺乳瓶
honyūbin
bottle

外出 gaishutsu・going out

ベビーカー
bebīkā
stroller

フード
fūdo
hood

乳母車
ubaguruma
baby carriage

おむつ
omutsu
diaper

キャリーコット
kyarīkotto
infant carrier

おむつ替えバッグ
omutsu kae baggu
diaper bag

ベビースリング
bebī suringu
baby sling

ユティリティルーム yutiriti rūmu • utility room

洗濯 sentaku • laundry

洗濯物
sentakumono
clean clothes

汚れ物
yogoremono
dirty washing

洗濯物入れ
sentakumono ire
laundry basket

洗濯機
sentakki
washing machine

洗濯乾燥機
sentaku kansōki
washer-dryer

乾燥機
kansōki
tumble dryer

洗濯かご
sentakukago
laundry basket

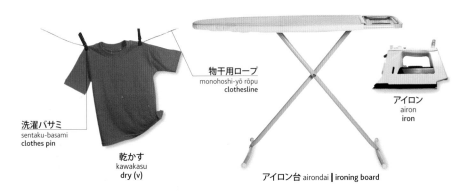

物干用ロープ
monohoshi-yō rōpu
clothesline

アイロン
airon
iron

洗濯バサミ
sentaku-basami
clothes pin

乾かす
kawakasu
dry (v)

アイロン台 airondai | **ironing board**

関連用語 kanrenyōgo • vocabulary

（汚れ物を洗濯機に）入れる
(yogoremono o sentakki ni) ireru
load (v)

脱水する
dassui suru
spin (v)

アイロンをかける
airon o kakeru
iron (v)

この洗濯機は、どうやって使うのですか。
kono sentakki wa dōyatte tsukaunodesuka?
How do I operate the washing machine?

濯ぐ
susugu
rinse (v)

脱水機
dassuiki
spin dryer

柔軟仕上げ剤
jūnan shiagezai
fabric softener

色物／白系の設定は何ですか。
iromono/shirokei no settei wa nandesuka?
What is the setting for colors/whites?

掃除道具 sōji dōgu • cleaning equipment

吸い込みホース
suikomi hōsu
suction hose

ブラシ
burashi
brush

ちりとり
chiritori
dustpan

漂白剤
hyōhakuzai
bleach

バケツ
baketsu
bucket

粉末洗剤
funmatsu senzai
powder

液体洗剤
ekitai senzai
liquid

ダスター
dasutā
dustcloth

掃除機
sōjiki
vacuum cleaner

モップ
moppu
mop

洗剤
senzai
detergent

艶出し剤
tsuyadashizai
polish

掃除 sōji • activities

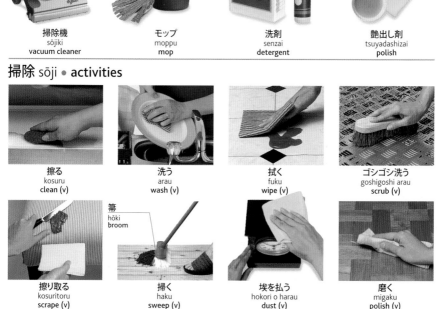

擦る
kosuru
clean (v)

洗う
arau
wash (v)

拭く
fuku
wipe (v)

ゴシゴシ洗う
goshigoshi arau
scrub (v)

箒
hōki
broom

擦り取る
kosuritoru
scrape (v)

掃く
haku
sweep (v)

埃を払う
hokori o harau
dust (v)

磨く
migaku
polish (v)

作業場 sagyōba • workshop

チャック
chakku
chuck

ドリルビット
doriru bitto
drill bit

電池パック
denchi pakku
battery pack

ジグソー
jigusō
jigsaw

充電式ドリル
jūden-shiki doriru
rechargeable drill

電気ドリル
denki doriru
electric drill

グルーガン
gurū gan
glue gun

クランプ
kurampu
clamp

鋸刃
nokogiri-ba
blade

万力
manriki
vice

サンダー
sandā
sander

丸鋸
marunoko
circular saw

作業台
sagyōdai
workbench

木工用接着剤
mokkō-yō setchakuzai
wood glue

工具棚
kōgu-dana
tool rack

ルーター
rūtā
router

ハンドドリル
hando doriru
bit brace

鉋屑
kannakuzu
wood shavings

延長コード
enchō kōdo
extension cord

テクニック tekunikku · **techniques**

切る
kiru
cut (v)

（鋸で）切る
(nokogiri de) kiru
saw (v)

穴をあける
ana o akeru
drill (v)

（金槌で）打つ
(kanazuchi de) utsu
hammer (v)

鉋をかける kanna o kakeru
plane (v)

旋盤加工する
sembankakō suru | **turn (v)**

削る kezuru | **carve (v)**

半田
handa
solder

半田付けする
handazuke suru | **solder (v)**

材料 zairyō · **materials**

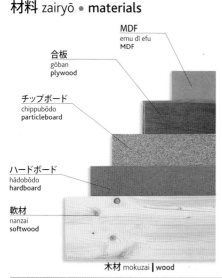

合板
gōban
plywood

MDF
emu dī efu
MDF

チップボード
chippubōdo
particleboard

ハードボード
hādobōdo
hardboard

軟材
nanzai
softwood

木材 mokuzai | **wood**

硬材
kōzai
hardwood

ニス
nisu
varnish

木材着色剤
mokuzai
chakushokuzai
woodstain

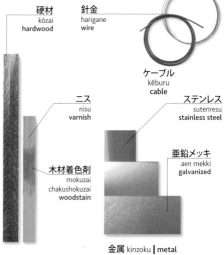

針金
harigane
wire

ケーブル
kēburu
cable

ステンレス
sutenresu
stainless steel

亜鉛メッキ
aen mekki
galvanized

金属 kinzoku | **metal**

道具箱 dōgubako • toolbox

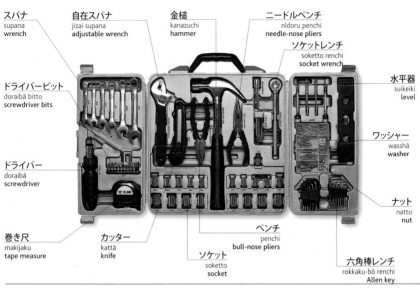

スパナ
supana
wrench

自在スパナ
jizai supana
adjustable wrench

金槌
kanazuchi
hammer

ニードルペンチ
nidoru penchi
needle-nose pliers

ソケットレンチ
soketto renchi
socket wrench

水平器
suikeiki
level

ドライバービット
doraibā bitto
screwdriver bits

ワッシャー
wasshā
washer

ドライバー
doraibā
screwdriver

ナット
natto
nut

巻き尺
makijaku
tape measure

カッター
kattā
knife

ソケット
soketto
socket

ペンチ
penchi
bull-nose pliers

六角棒レンチ
rokkaku-bō renchi
Allen key

ドリルビット doriru bitto • **drill bits**

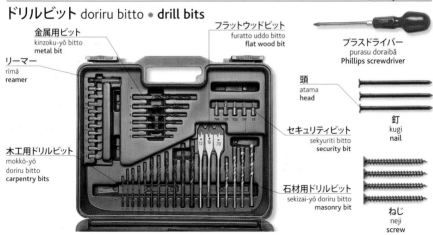

金属用ビット
kinzoku-yō bitto
metal bit

フラットウッドビット
furatto uddo bitto
flat wood bit

プラスドライバー
purasu doraibā
Phillips screwdriver

リーマー
rīmā
reamer

頭
atama
head

釘
kugi
nail

木工用ドリルビット
mokkō-yō
doriru bitto
carpentry bits

セキュリティビット
sekyuriti bitto
security bit

石材用ドリルビット
sekizai-yō doriru bitto
masonry bit

ねじ
neji
screw

ワイヤーストリッパー
waiyā sutorippā
wire strippers

ワイヤーカッター
waiyā kattā
wire cutters

半田ごて
handagote
soldering iron

絶縁テープ
zetsuen tēpu
electrical tape

カッターナイフ
kattā naifu
scalpel

糸鋸
itonoko
fretsaw

半田
handa
solder

胴付き鋸 dōtsuki noko | tenon saw

保護めがね
hogo megane
safety goggles

鉋
kanna
plane

手引き鋸
tebiki noko
handsaw

マイターボックス
maitā bokkusu
miter block

弓鋸
yuminoko
hacksaw

ハンドドリル
hand odoriru
hand drill

スチールウール
suchīru'ūru
steel wool

レンチ
renchi
wrench

鑿
nomi
chisel

紙やすり
kami yasuri
sandpaper

吸引カップ
kyūin kappu
plunger

やすり
yasuri
file

砥石
toishi
sharpening stone

パイプカッター paipu kattā | pipe cutter

内装工事 naisō kōji • decorating

鋏
hasami
scissors

クラフトナイフ
kurafuto naifu
utility knife

下げ振り
sagefuri
plumb line

スクレーパー
sukurēpā
scraper

内装工事職人
naisō kōji shokunin
decorator

壁紙
kabegami
wallpaper

脚立
kyatatsu
stepladder

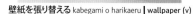

壁紙刷毛
kabegami-bake
wallpaper brush

糊付け台
nori-zuke dai
pasting table

糊刷毛
noribake
pasting brush

壁紙用糊
kabegami-yō nori
wallpaper paste

バケツ
baketsu
bucket

壁紙を張り替える kabegami o harikaeru | wallpaper (v)

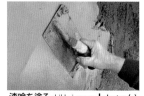

剥がす hagasu | strip (v)

埋める umeru | fill (v)

研磨する kenma suru | sand (v)

漆喰を塗る shikkui o nuru | plaster (v)

壁紙を貼る kabegami o haru | hang (v)

タイルを貼る tairu o haru | tile (v)

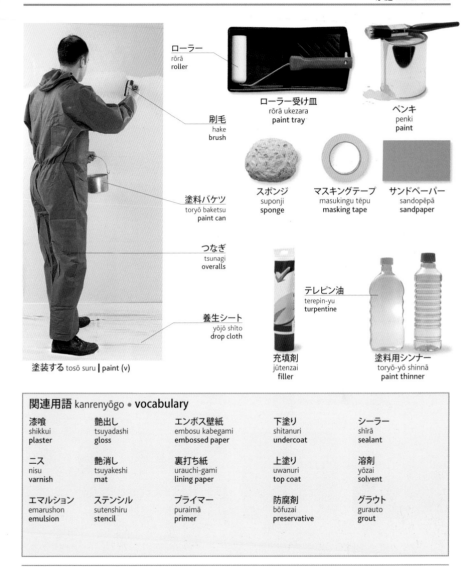

ローラー
rōrā
roller

ローラー受け皿
rōrā ukezara
paint tray

ペンキ
penki
paint

刷毛
hake
brush

スポンジ
suponji
sponge

マスキングテープ
masukingu tēpu
masking tape

サンドペーパー
sandopēpā
sandpaper

塗料バケツ
toryō baketsu
paint can

つなぎ
tsunagi
overalls

テレピン油
terepin-yu
turpentine

養生シート
yōjō shīto
drop cloth

充填剤
jūtenzai
filler

塗料用シンナー
toryō-yō shinnā
paint thinner

塗装する tosō suru | paint (v)

関連用語 kanrenyōgo • vocabulary

漆喰 shikkui **plaster**	艶出し tsuyadashi **gloss**	エンボス壁紙 embosu kabegami **embossed paper**	下塗り shitanuri **undercoat**	シーラー shīrā **sealant**
ニス nisu **varnish**	艶消し tsuyakeshi **mat**	裏打ち紙 urauchi-gami **lining paper**	上塗り uwanuri **top coat**	溶剤 yōzai **solvent**
エマルション emarushon **emulsion**	ステンシル sutenshiru **stencil**	プライマー puraimā **primer**	防腐剤 bōfuzai **preservative**	グラウト gurauto **grout**

庭 niwa • garden

庭の様式 niwa no yōshiki • garden styles

テラスガーデン terasu gāden | patio garden

フォーマルな庭園 fōmaru-na teien | formal garden

コテージガーデン
kotēji gāden
cottage garden

ハーブ園
hābu-en
herb garden

屋上庭園
okujō teien
roof garden

石庭
sekitei
rock garden

中庭 nakaniwa | courtyard

ウォーターガーデン
wōtā gāden
water garden

庭のアクセント
niwa no akusento
• garden features

ハンギングバスケット
hangingu basuketto
hanging basket

トレリス torerisu | trellis

パーゴラ
pāgora
arbor

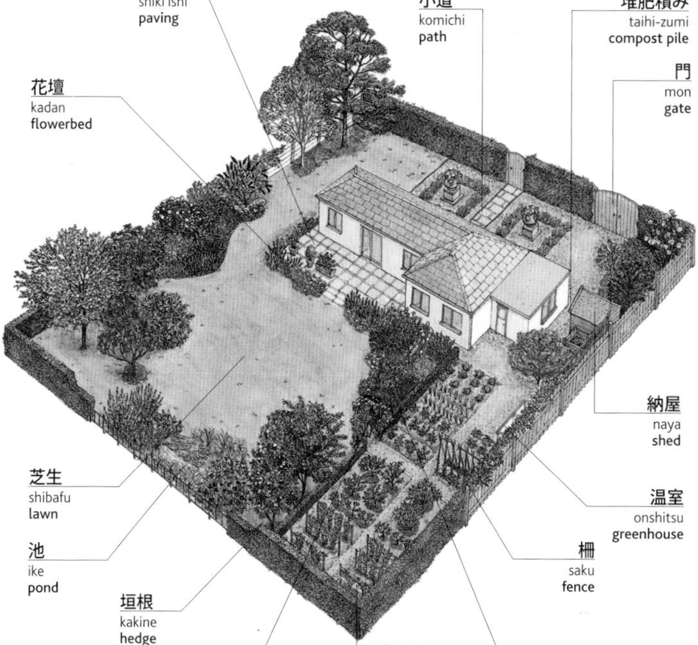

土壌 dojō
● soil

敷石
shiki'ishi
paving

小道
komichi
path

堆肥積み
taihi-zumi
compost pile

門
mon
gate

花壇
kadan
flowerbed

納屋
naya
shed

温室
onshitsu
greenhouse

柵
saku
fence

芝生
shibafu
lawn

池
ike
pond

垣根
kakine
hedge

アーチ
āchi
arch

家庭菜園
katei saien
vegetable garden

ハーブのボーダー花壇
hābu no bōdā kadan
herbaceous border

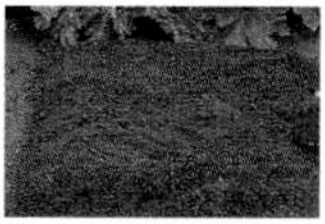

表土
hyōdo
topsoil

砂土
sunatsuchi
sand

石灰質土壌
sekkai-shitsu dojō
chalk

沈泥
chindei
silt

粘土
nendo
clay

デッキ
dekki
deck

噴水 funsui | fountain

庭の植物 niwa no shokubutsu • garden plants

植物の種類 shokubutsu no shurui • types of plants

一年草
ichinensō
annual

二年草
ninensō
biennial

多年草
tanensō
perennial

球根植物
kyūkon shokubutsu
bulb

シダ
shida
fern

い草
igusa
rush

竹
take
bamboo

雑草
zassō
weed

ハーブ
hābu
herb

水草
mizukusa
water plant

木
ki
tree

椰子の木
yashi no ki
palm

針葉樹
shin'yōju
conifer

常緑樹
jōryokuju
evergreen

落葉樹
rakuyōju
deciduous

トピアリー
topiarī
topiary

高山植物
kōzan shokubutsu
alpine

多肉植物
taniku shokubutsu
succulent

サボテン
saboten
cactus

植木
ueki
potted plant

陰性植物
insei shokubutsu
shade plant

蔓性植物
tsurusei shokubutsu
climber

顕花性低木
kenkasei teiboku
flowering shrub

グランドカバー
gurando kabā
ground cover

匍匐植物
hofuku shokubutsu
creeper

観葉植物
kan'yō
shokubutsu
ornamental

草
kusa
grass

園芸用品 engei yōhin • garden tools

堆肥
taihi
compost

種
tane
seeds

骨粉
kotsufun
bone meal

砂利
jari
gravel

熊手
kumade
lawn rake

ショベル
shoberu
spade

フォーク
fōku
fork

雑草刈り鋏
zassō kari-basami
long-handled shears

レーキ
rēki
rake

鍬
kuwa
hoe

集草バッグ
shūsō baggu
grass bag

モーター
mōtā
motor

取っ手
totte
handle

トラグ
toragu
trug

シールド
shīrudo
shield

トリマー
torimā
trimmer

芝刈り機
shibakariki
lawnmower

スタンド
sutando
stand

一輪台車
ichirin daisha
wheelbarrow

ハンドフォーク
hando fōku
hand fork

スコップ
sukoppu
trowel

剪定鋏
sentei-basami
pruners

園芸用手袋
engei-yō tebukuro
gardening gloves

刃
ha
blade

種蒔きトレイ
tanemaki torei
seed tray

結束紐
kessoku himo
twine

ラベル
raberu
labels

ビニールタイ
binīru tai
twist ties

リングタイ
ringu tai
ring ties

刈り込み鋏
karikomi-basami
shears

支え棒
sasaebō
stakes

篩
furui
sieve

剪定鋸
sentei noko
hand saw

殺虫剤
satchūzai
pesticide

植木鉢
uekibachi
plant pot

ゴム長靴
gomunagagutsu
rubber boots

水やり mizuyari · watering

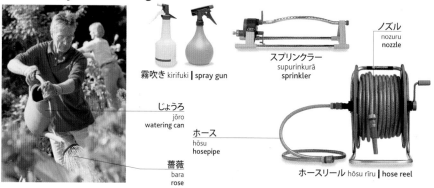

霧吹き kirifuki | spray gun

スプリンクラー
supurinkurā
sprinkler

ノズル
nozuru
nozzle

じょうろ
jōro
watering can

ホース
hōsu
hosepipe

薔薇
bara
rose

ホースリール hōsu rīru | hose reel

園芸 engei • gardening

芝生
shibafu
lawn

垣根
kakine
hedge

花壇
kadan
flowerbed

杭
kui
stake

芝刈り機
shibakariki
lawnmower

芝刈りする shibakari suru | mow (v)

芝で覆う
shiba de ôu
sod (v)

刺す
sasu
spike (v)

掃く
haku
rake (v)

刈り込む
karikomu
trim (v)

掘る
horu
dig (v)

種を植える
tane o ueru
sow (v)

追肥する
tsuihi suru
top-dress (v)

水をやる
mizu o yaru
water (v)

整枝する
seishi suru
train (v)

（終わった花を）摘み取る
(owatta hana o) tsumitoru
deadhead (v)

噴霧する
funmu suru
spray (v)

支え棒
sasaebō
stake

接ぎ木する
tsugiki suru
graft (v)

切り枝
kirieda
cutting

枝分けする
edawake suru
propagate (v)

剪定する
sentei suru
prune (v)

（支えに）繋ぐ
(sasae ni) tsunagu
stake (v)

植え替える
ue-kaeru
transplant (v)

除草する
josō suru
weed (v)

根覆いする
neōi suru
mulch (v)

収穫する
shūkaku suru
harvest (v)

関連用語 kanrenyōgo • vocabulary

栽培する saibai suru **cultivate (v)**	造園する zōen suru **landscape (v)**	肥料をやる hiryō o yaru **fertilize (v)**	篩にかける furui ni kakeru **sieve (v)**	有機 yūki **organic**	苗 nae **seedling**	心土 shindo **subsoil**
手入れする teire suru **tend (v)**	（大きな鉢に）植え替える (ōkina hachi ni) ue-kaeru **pot up (v)**	摘む tsumu **pick (v)**	空気に曝す kūki ni sarasu **aerate (v)**	排水 haisui **drainage**	肥料 hiryō **fertilizer**	除草剤 josōzai **weedkiller**

職務 shokumu
services

緊急サービス kinkyū sābisu • emergency services

救急車 kyūkyūsha • ambulance

担架
tanka
stretcher

救急車 kyūkyūsha | ambulance

救急医療隊員 kyūkyū iryō tai'in
paramedic

警察 keisatsu • police

バッジ
bajji
badge

制服
seifuku
uniform

サイレン
sairen
siren

警光灯
keikōtō
lights

警棒
keibō
nightstick

拳銃
kenjū
gun

手錠
tejō
handcuffs

警官 keikan | police officer

パトカー
patokā
police car

警察署
keisatsusho
police station

関連用語 kanrenyōgo • vocabulary

警部 keibu lieutenant	容疑者 yōgisha suspect	申し立て mōshitate complaint	逮捕 taiho arrest
犯罪 hanzai crime	暴行 bōkō assault	調査 chōsa investigation	留置場 ryūchijō jail cell
刑事 keiji detective	指紋 shimon fingerprint	押し込み強盗 oshikomi gōtō burglary	告訴 kokuso charge

消防隊 shōbōtai • fire department

ヘルメット
herumetto
helmet

煙
kemuri
smoke

ホース
hōsu
hose

消防士
shōbōshi
firefighters

バスケット
basuketto
cradle

水ジェット
mizu jetto
water jet

運転台
untendai
cab

腕
ude
boom

梯子
hashigo
ladder

火事 kaji | fire

消防署
shōbōsho
fire station

非常階段
hijō kaidan
fire escape

消防車
shōbōsha
fire engine

煙報知器
kemuri hōchiki
smoke alarm

火災警報機
kasai keihōki
fire alarm

防災斧
bōsai ono
ax

消化器
shōkaki
fire extinguisher

消火栓
shōkasen
hydrant

警察／消防車／救急車が必要です。
keisatsu/shōbōsha/kyūkyūsha ga hitsuyō desu.
I need the police/fire department/ ambulance.

...で火が出ています。
... de hi ga dete imasu.
There's a fire at...

事故がありました。
jiko ga arimashita.
There's been an accident.

警察を呼んでください。
keisatsu o yonde kudasai!
Call the police!

銀行 ginkō • bank

客
kyaku
customer

窓口
madoguchi
window

出納係
suitō-gakari
cashier

リーフレット
rīfuretto
brochures

カウンター
kauntā
counter

入金書
nyūkin-sho
deposit slips

デビットカード
debitto kādo
debit card

半券
hanken
stub

口座番号
kōza bangō
account number

署名
shomei
signature

金額
kingaku
amount

支店長
shitenchō
bank manager

クレジットカード
kurejitto kādo
credit card

小切手帳
kogitte-chō
checkbook

小切手
kogitte
check

関連用語 kanrenyōgo • vocabulary

貯金 chokin **savings**	住宅ローン jūtaku rōn **mortgage**	支払い shiharai **payment**	入金する nyūkin suru **deposit (v)**	当座預金口座 tōzayokin kōza **checking account**
税 zei **tax**	超過引き出し chōka hikidashi **overdraft**	自動引き落とし jidō hikiotoshi **automatic payment**	銀行手数料 ginkō tesūryō **fee**	普通預金口座 futsūyokin kōza **savings account**
ローン rōn **loan**	金利 kinri **interest rate**	出金依頼書 shukkin irai-sho **withdrawal slip**	銀行振込 ginkō furikomi **electronic transfer**	暗証番号 anshō bangō **PIN**

硬貨
köka
coin

紙幣
shihei
bill

金銭 kinsen | money

画面
gamen
screen

キーパッド
kïpaddo
keypad

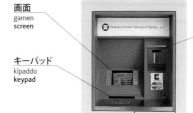

カード挿入口
kādo sōnyū-guchi
card slot

ATM ē tī emu | ATM

外貨 gaika • foreign currency

両替所
ryōgaejo
bureau de change

旅行小切手
ryokō kogitte
traveler's check

換算率
kansan ritsu
exchange rate

金融 kin'yū • finance

株価
kabuka
share price

ブローカー
burōkā
stockbroker

金融アドバイザー
kin'yū adobaizā
financial advisor

証券取引所 shōken torihiki-jo
stock exchange

関連用語 kanrenyōgo • vocabulary

換金する
kankin suru
cash (v)

株
kabu
shares

額面金額
gakumen kingaku
denomination

配当
haitō
dividends

手数料
tesūryō
commission

会計士
kaikeishi
accountant

投資
tōshi
investment

ポートフォリオ
pōtoforio
portfolio

株式
kabushiki
stocks

エクイティ
ekuiti
equity

これを両替できますか。
kore o ryōgae dekimasuka?
May I change this please?

今日の換算率は何ですか。
kyō no kansan ritsu wa nandesuka?
What is today's exchange rate?

コミュニケーション komyunikēshon · **communications**

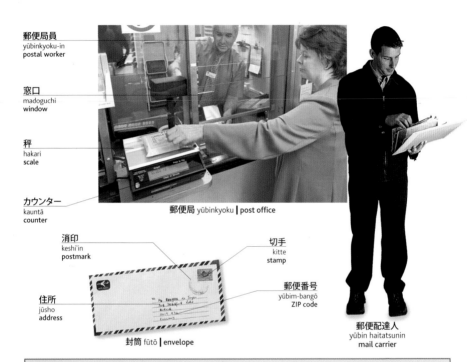

郵便局員
yūbinkyoku-in
postal worker

窓口
madoguchi
window

秤
hakari
scale

カウンター
kauntā
counter

郵便局 yūbinkyoku | **post office**

消印
keshi'in
postmark

切手
kitte
stamp

住所
jūsho
address

郵便番号
yūbim-bangō
ZIP code

封筒 fūtō | **envelope**

郵便配達人
yūbin haitatsunin
mail carrier

関連用語 kanrenyōgo · **vocabulary**

手紙 tegami **letter**	**差出人住所** sashidashinin jūsho **return address**	**配達** haitatsu **delivery**	**壊れ物** kowaremono **fragile**	**折曲厳禁** orimage genkin **do not bend (v)**
航空便 kōkūbin **by airmail**	**署名** shomei **signature**	**郵便為替** yūbin kawase **money order**	**郵便袋** yūbim-bukuro **mailbag**	**こちらが上** kochira ga ue **this way up**
書留郵便 kakitome yūbin **registered mail**	**集荷** shūka **pickup**	**郵送料** yūsō-ryō **postage**	**電報** dempō **telegram**	**ファクス** fakusu **fax**

郵便ポスト
yūbin posuto
mailbox

郵便受け
yūbin-uke
letter slot

小包
kozutsumi
package

宅配
takuhai
courier

電話 denwa ・ telephone

受話器
juwaki
handset

ベース
bēsu
base station

コードレス電話
kōdoresu denwa
cordless phone

留守番電話
rusuban denwa
answering machine

ビデオ電話
bideo denwa
video phone

公衆電話ボックス
kōshū-denwa bokkusu
telephone box

キーパッド
kīpaddo
keypad

携帯電話
keitai denwa
cell phone

受話器
juwaki
receiver

おつり
otsuri
coin return

硬貨式公衆電話
kōka-shiki kōshū-denwa
coin phone

カード式公衆電話
kādo-shiki kōshū-denwa
card phone

関連用語 kanrenyōgo ・ vocabulary

番号案内 bangō annai **directory assistance**	**電話に出る** denwa ni deru **answer (v)**	**交換手** kōkanshu **operator**	**...の電話番号を教えてください。** ... no denwa bangō o oshiete kudasai. **Please give me the number for...**
コレクトコール korekuto kōru **collect call**	**携帯メール** keitai mēru **text message**	**通話中** tsūwa-chū **busy**	**...の局番は何ですか。** ... no kyokuban wa nandesuka? **What is the area code for...?**
電話する denwa suru **dial (v)**	**音声メッセージ** onsei messēji **voice message**	**不通** futsū **disconnected**	

ホテル hoteru · hotel
ロビー robī · lobby

宿泊客
shukuhaku kyaku
guest

部屋の鍵
heya no kagi
room key

メッセージ
messēji
messages

分類棚
bunrui-dana
pigeonhole

フロント係
furonto-gakari
receptionist

宿泊者名簿
shukuhaku-
sha meibo
register

カウンター
kauntā
counter

フロント furonto | reception

荷物
nimotsu
luggage

カート
kāto
cart

ポーター pōtā | porter

エレベーター erebētā | elevator

部屋番号
heya bangō
room number

客室 kyakushitsu · rooms

シングルルーム
shinguru rūmu
single room

ダブルルーム
daburu rūmu
double room

ツインルーム
tsuin rūmu
twin room

客室付きバスルーム
kyakushitsu-zuki basurūmu
private bathroom

職務 shokumu • services

掃除サービス
sōji sābisu
maid service

洗濯サービス
sentaku sābisu
laundry service

朝食トレイ
chōshoku torei
breakfast tray

ルームサービス rūmu sābisu | room service

ミニバー
minibā
minibar

レストラン
restoran
restaurant

ジム
jimu
gym

プール
pūru
swimming pool

関連用語 kanrenyōgo • vocabulary

朝食付き
chōshoku-tsuki
bed and breakfast

3食付き
sanshoku-tsuki
all meals included

2食付き
nishoku-tsuki
some meals included

空室はありますか。
kūshitsu wa arimasuka?
Do you have any vacancies?

予約してあります。
yoyaku shite arimasu.
I have a reservation.

シングルルームをお願いします。
shinguru rūmu o onegai shimasu.
I'd like a single room.

3泊お願いします。
sampaku onegai shimasu.
I'd like a room for three nights.

一泊いくらですか。
ippaku ikura desuka?
What is the charge per night?

チェックアウトは何時ですか。
chekkuauto wa nanji desuka?
When do I have to vacate the room?

買い物 kaimono
shopping

ショッピングセンター shoppingu sentā • shopping center

アトリウム
atoriumu
atrium

看板
kamban
sign

エレベーター
erebētā
elevator

3階
sangai
second floor

2階
nikai
first floor

エスカレーター
esukarētā
escalator

1階
ikkai
ground floor

客
kyaku
customer

関連用語 kanrenyōgo • vocabulary

子供用品売場
kodomo yōhin uriba
children's department

鞄売場
kaban uriba
luggage department

靴売場
kutsu uriba
shoe department

売場案内
uriba annai
store directory

店員
ten'in
sales clerk

カスタマーサービス
kasutamā sābisu
customer services

試着室
shichaku shitsu
fitting rooms

ベビールーム
bebī rūmu
baby changing facilities

お手洗い
o-tearai
restrooms

これは、いくらですか。
kore wa ikura desuka?
How much is this?

これを交換できますか。
kore o kōkan dekimasuka?
May I exchange this?

デパート depāto ● department store

紳士服
shinshi fuku
men's wear

婦人服
fujin fuku
women's wear

ランジェリー
ranjerī
lingerie

香水売場
kōsui uriba
perfume

化粧品
keshōhin
beauty

寝具・タオル類
shingu taoru rui
bed and bath

家具
kagu
home furnishings

小間物
komamono
notions

台所用品
daidokoro yōhin
kitchenware

陶磁器
tōjiki
china

電気製品
denki seihin
electronics

照明器具
shōmei kigu
lighting

スポーツ用品
supōtsu yōhin
sporting goods

玩具
omocha
toys

文房具
bumbōgu
stationery

食品売場
shokuhin uriba
groceries

スーパーマーケット sūpāmāketto • supermarket

ベルトコンベア
beruto kombea
conveyer belt

レジ係　特売品
reji-gakari　tokubaihin
cashier　**specials**

通路
tsūro
aisle

棚
tana
shelf

チェックアウト chekkuauto | **checkout**

客
kyaku
customer

レジ
reji
cash register

買い物袋
kaimono-bukuro
shopping bag

食料品
shokuryōhin
groceries

取っ手
totte
handle

780863 185779

バーコード
bākōdo
bar code

カート kāto | **cart**

籠 kago | **basket**

バーコード読み取り装置 bākōdo
yomitori sōchi | **scanner**

パン類
pan rui
bakery

乳製品
nyūseihin
dairy

シリアル食品
shiriaru shokuhin
breakfast cereals

缶詰
kanzume
canned food

菓子類
kashi rui
confectionery

野菜
yasai
vegetables

果物
kudamono
fruit

肉
niku
meat and poultry

魚
sakana
fish

デリカテッセン
derikatessen
deli

冷凍食品
reitō shokuhin
frozen food

インスタント食品
insutanto shokuhin
convenience food

飲物
nomimono
drinks

家庭用品
katei yōhin
household products

化粧品
keshōhin
toiletries

ベビー用品
bebī yōhin
baby products

電気製品
denki seihin
electrical goods

ペットフード
petto fūdo
pet food

雑誌 zasshi | magazines

薬局 yakkyoku • drugstore

歯磨き用品
hamigaki yōhin
dental care

生理用品
seiri yōhin
**feminine
hygiene**

デオドラント
deodoranto
deodorants

ビタミン剤
bitamin-zai
vitamins

調剤室
chōzai shitsu
pharmacy

薬剤師
yakuzaishi
pharmacist

咳止め
sekidome
cough medicine

薬草剤
yakusō-zai
herbal remedies

スキンケア
sukinkea
skin care

アフターサンケア
afutāsankea
aftersun

サンスクリーン
sansukurīn
sunscreen

日焼け止め
hiyakedome
sunblock

虫除け
mushiyoke
insect repellent

ウェットティッシュ
wetto tisshu
wet wipe

ティッシュ
tisshu
tissue

生理用ナプキン
seiri-yō napukin
sanitary napkin

タンポン
tampon
tampon

パンティライナー
panti rainā
panty liner

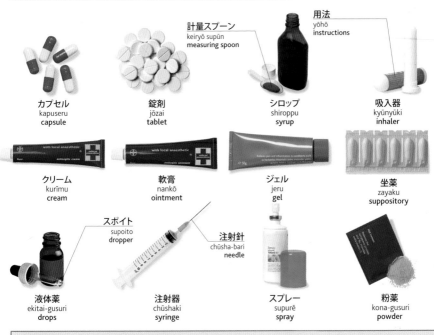

計量スプーン
keiryō supūn
measuring spoon

用法
yōhō
instructions

カプセル
kapuseru
capsule

錠剤
jōzai
tablet

シロップ
shiroppu
syrup

吸入器
kyūnyūki
inhaler

クリーム
kurīmu
cream

軟膏
nankō
ointment

ジェル
jeru
gel

坐薬
zayaku
suppository

スポイト
supoito
dropper

注射針
chūsha-bari
needle

液体薬
ekitai-gusuri
drops

注射器
chūshaki
syringe

スプレー
supurē
spray

粉薬
kona-gusuri
powder

関連用語 kanrenyōgo • vocabulary

鉄分
tetsubun
iron

インスリン
insurin
insulin

使い捨て
tsukaisute
disposable

医薬品
iyakuhin
medicine

痛み止め
itamidome
analgesic

カルシウム
karushiumu
calcium

副作用
fukusayō
side-effects

水溶性
suiyōsei
soluble

下剤
gezai
laxative

鎮静剤
chinsei-zai
sedative

マグネシウム
maguneshiumu
magnesium

使用期限
shiyō kigen
expiration date

用量
yōryō
dosage

下痢
geri
diarrhea

睡眠薬
suimin'yaku
sleeping pill

マルチビタミン
maruchi bitamin
multivitamins

酔い止め
yoidome
travel sickness pills

投薬
tōyaku
medication

のど飴
nodo ame
sore throat lozenge

抗炎症剤
kōenshō-zai
antiinflammatory

花屋 hanaya ● florist

花
hana
flowers

グラジオラス
gurajiorasu
gladiolus

百合
yuri
lily

菖蒲
ayame
iris

アカシア
akashia
acacia

ひな菊
hinagiku
daisy

菊
kiku
chrysanthemum

カーネーション
kānēshon
carnation

かすみ草
kasumisō
gypsophila

植木
ueki
potted plant

アラセイトウ
araseitō
stocks

ガーベラ
gābera
gerbera

群葉
gun'yō
foliage

薔薇
bara
roses

フリージア
furījia
freesia

花瓶
kabin
vase

蘭
ran
orchid

牡丹
botan
peony

花束
hanataba
bunch

茎
kuki
stem

水仙
suisen
daffodil

蕾
tsubomi
bud

包装紙
hōsō-shi
wrapping

チューリップ chūrippu | tulip

アレンジメント arenjimento ● arrangements

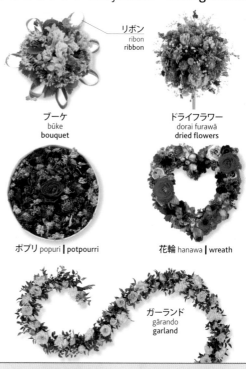

リボン
ribon
ribbon

ブーケ
būke
bouquet

ドライフラワー
dorai furawā
dried flowers

ポプリ popuri | potpourri

花輪 hanawa | wreath

ガーランド
gārando
garland

メッセージを付けてください。
messēji o tsukete kudasai?
Can I attach a message?

包んでください。
tsutsunde kudasai?
Can I have them wrapped?

...に送っていただけますか。
... ni okutte itadakemasuka?
Can you send them to...?

何日ぐらい保ちますか。
nannichi gurai tamochimasuka?
How long will these last?

香りがしますか。
kaori ga shimasuka?
Are they fragrant?

...の花束をください。
... no hanataba o kudasai?
Can I have a bunch of... please?

新聞販売店 shimbun hambaiten ● **newsstand**

煙草
tabako
cigarettes

煙草一箱
tabako hitohako
pack of cigarettes

マッチ
matchi
matches

宝くじ
takarakuji
lottery tickets

切手
kitte
stamps

絵葉書
ehagaki
postcard

漫画本
manga-bon
comic book

雑誌
zasshi
magazine

新聞
shimbun
newspaper

喫煙 kitsuen ● **smoking**

刻み煙草
kizami tabako
tobacco

ライター
raitā
lighter

ステム
sutemu
stem

ボウル
bo-uru
bowl

パイプ
paipu
pipe

葉巻
hamaki
cigar

菓子屋 kashiya • confectioner

箱詰めチョコレート
hakozume chokorēto
box of chocolates

チョコバー
chokobā
snack bar

ポテトチップス
poteto chippusu
chips

飴屋 ameya | sweet shop

関連用語 kanrenyōgo • vocabulary

ミルクチョコレート
miruku chokorēto
milk chocolate

キャラメル
kyarameru
caramel

スイートチョコレート
suīto chokorēto
dark chocolate

トラッフル
toraffuru
truffle

ホワイトチョコレート
howaito chokorēto
white chocolate

クッキー
kukkī
cookie

ピックンミックス
pikkunmikkusu
pick-and-mix

飴
ame
hard candy

菓子 kashi • candy

チョコレート
chokorēto
chocolate

板チョコ
itachoko
chocolate bar

飴
ame
candies

棒付きキャンディー
bō-tsuki kyandī
lollipop

トフィー tofī | toffee

ヌガー
nugā | nougat

マシュマロ
mashumaro
marshmallow

ハッカ飴
hakka ame
mint

ガム
gamu
chewing gum

ゼリービーンズ
zerībīnzu
jellybean

フルーツガム
furūtsu gamu
gum drop

甘草飴
kanzō ame
licorice

その他の店 sonota no mise ● other stores

パン屋
pan'ya
bakery

ケーキ屋
kēkiya
pastry shop

肉屋
nikuya
butcher shop

魚屋
sakanaya
fish store

八百屋
yaoya
greengrocer

食料品店
shokuryōhin-ten
grocery store

靴屋
kutsuya
shoe store

金物屋
kanamonoya
hardware store

骨董屋
kottōya
antique shop

ギフトショップ
gifuto shoppu
gift shop

旅行代理店
ryokō dairiten
travel agency

宝石店
hōseki-ten
jewelry store

本屋
hon'ya
bookstore

レコード店
rekōdo-ten
record store

酒屋
sakaya
liquor store

ペットショップ
petto shoppu
pet store

家具屋
kaguya
furniture store

ブティック
butikku
boutique

関連用語 kanrenyōgo • vocabulary

不動産屋
fudōsan-ya
real estate agency

カメラ屋
kamera-ya
camera store

園芸センター
engei sentā
garden center

健康食品店
kenkō shokuhin-ten
health food store

クリーニング屋
kurīningu-ya
dry cleaner's

画材屋
gazai-ya
art supply store

コインランドリー
koin randorī
laundromat

中古販売店
chūko hambai-ten
secondhand store

仕立屋
shitateya
tailor

美容院
biyōin
salon

市場 ichiba | **market**

食べ物 tabemono
food

肉 niku ● meat

ラム肉
ramu niku
lamb

肉屋
nikuya
butcher

肉フック
niku fukku
meat hook

秤
hakari
scale

研ぎ棒
togi-bō
knife sharpener

ベーコン
bēkon
bacon

ソーセージ
sōsēji
sausages

レバー
rebā
liver

関連用語 kanrenyōgo ● vocabulary

豚肉
butaniku
pork

鹿肉
shika niku
venison

内蔵
naizō
offal

放し飼いの
hanashigai no
free range

調理済み肉
chōri-zumi niku
cooked meat

牛肉
gyūniku
beef

ウサギ肉
usagi niku
rabbit

保存処理
hozon shori
cured

有機性
yūki-sei
organic

白身肉
shiromi niku
white meat

子牛肉
ko-ushi niku
veal

タン
tan
tongue

薫製
kunsei
smoked

低脂肪肉
teishibō niku
lean meat

赤身肉
akami niku
red meat

切り身 kirimi • cuts

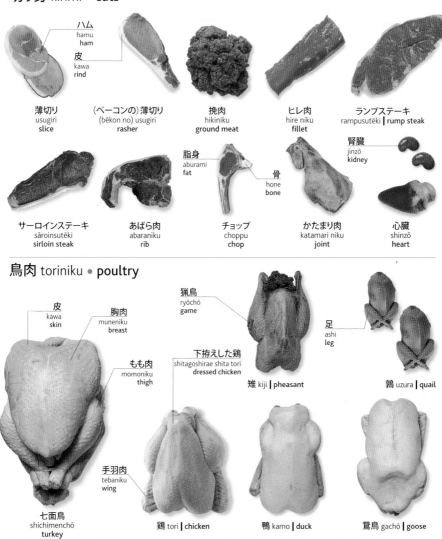

薄切り
usugiri
slice

（ベーコンの）薄切り
(bēkon no) usugiri
rasher

ハム
hamu
ham

皮
kawa
rind

挽肉
hikiniku
ground meat

ヒレ肉
hire niku
fillet

ランプステーキ
rampusutēki | **rump steak**

サーロインステーキ
sāroinsutēki
sirloin steak

あばら肉
abaraniku
rib

脂身
aburami
fat

チョップ
choppu
chop

骨
hone
bone

かたまり肉
katamari niku
joint

腎臓
jinzō
kidney

心臓
shinzō
heart

鳥肉 toriniku • poultry

皮
kawa
skin

胸肉
muneniku
breast

猟鳥
ryōchō
game

足
ashi
leg

もも肉
momoniku
thigh

下拵えした鶏
shitagoshirae shita tori
dressed chicken

雉 kiji | **pheasant**

鶉 uzura | **quail**

手羽肉
tebaniku
wing

七面鳥
shichimenchō
turkey

鶏 tori | **chicken**

鴨 kamo | **duck**

鵞鳥 gachō | **goose**

魚 sakana ● fish

剝き海老
mukiebi
peeled shrimp

氷
kōri
ice

ヒメジ
himeji
red mullet

オヒョウの切り身
ohyō no kirimi
halibut fillets

虹鱒
nijimasu
rainbow trout

ガンギエイのヒレ
gangiei no hire
skate wings

魚屋
sakanaya
fishmonger's

アンコウ
ankō
monkfish

鯖
saba
mackerel

鱒
masu
trout

メカジキ
mekajiki
swordfish

ドーバーカレイ
dōbā karei
Dover sole

レモンガレイ
remon garei
lemon sole

コダラ
kodara
haddock

鰯
iwashi
sardine

ガンギエイ
gangiei
skate

ホワイティング
howaitingu
whiting

スズキ
suzuki
sea bass

鮭 sake | salmon

鱈
tara
cod

鯛
tai
sea bream

鮪
maguro
tuna

海産物 kaisambutsu・seafood

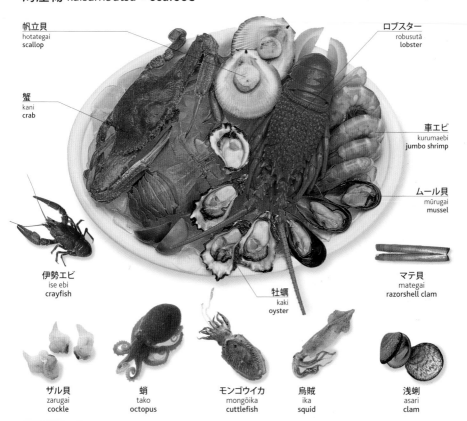

帆立貝
hotategai
scallop

ロブスター
robusutā
lobster

蟹
kani
crab

車エビ
kurumaebi
jumbo shrimp

ムール貝
mūrugai
mussel

伊勢エビ
ise ebi
crayfish

マテ貝
mategai
razorshell clam

牡蠣
kaki
oyster

ザル貝
zarugai
cockle

蛸
tako
octopus

モンゴウイカ
mongōika
cuttlefish

烏賊
ika
squid

浅蜊
asari
clam

関連用語 kanrenyōgo・vocabulary

冷凍	塩ふり	薫製	鱗を取った	切り身	厚切り	尾	骨	鱗	寿司	刺身
reitō	shio-furi	kunsei	uroko o totta	kirimi	atsu-giri	o	hone	uroko	sushi	sashimi
frozen	salted	smoked	descaled	fillet	loin	tail	bone	scale	sushi	sashimi

新鮮	腸を取った	皮を剥いた	骨を取った	おろした	筒切り	腸を取ってください。
shinsen	wata o totta	kawa o muita	hone o totta	oroshita	tsutsugiri	wata o totte kudasai?
fresh	cleaned	skinned	boned	filleted	steak	Will you clean it for me?

野菜1 yasai ● vegetables 1

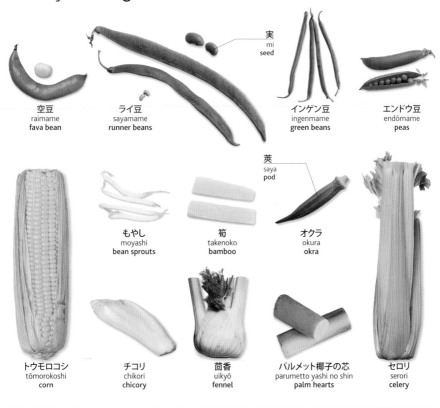

実
mi
seed

空豆
raimame
fava bean

ライ豆
sayamame
runner beans

インゲン豆
ingenmame
green beans

エンドウ豆
endōmame
peas

莢
saya
pod

もやし
moyashi
bean sprouts

筍
takenoko
bamboo

オクラ
okura
okra

トウモロコシ
tōmorokoshi
corn

チコリ
chikori
chicory

茴香
uikyō
fennel

パルメット椰子の芯
parumetto yashi no shin
palm hearts

セロリ
serori
celery

関連用語 kanrenyōgo ● vocabulary

白菜	茎	種	芯	有機野菜はありますか。
hakusai	kuki	tane	shin	yūki yasai wa arimasuka?
Chinese leaves	**stalk**	**kernel**	**heart**	**Do you sell organic vegetables?**
葉	房	先端	有機（栽培）	これは地元産ですか。
ha	fusa	sentan	yūki (saibai)	kore wa jimoto-san desuka?
leaf	**floret**	**tip**	**organic**	**Are these grown locally?**

ロケットサラダ
rokettosarada
arugula

クレソン
kureson
watercress

赤チコリ
aka chikori
radicchio

芽キャベツ
mekyabetsu
brussels sprouts

フダンソウ
fudansō
Swiss chard

ケール
kēru
kale

ギシギシ
gishigishi
sorrel

エンダイブ
endaibu
endive

タンポポ
tampopo
dandelion

ホウレン草
hōrensō
spinach

コールラビ
kōrurabi
kohlrabi

チンゲン菜
chingensai
bok choy

レタス
retasu
lettuce

ブロッコリ
burokkori
broccoli

キャベツ
kyabetsu
cabbage

新キャベツ
shin kyabetsu
spring greens

野菜2 yasai ● vegetables 2

カリフラワー
karifurawā
cauliflower

アーティチョーク
ātichōku
artichoke

ラディッシュ
radisshu
radish

カブ
kabu
turnip

ジャガイモ
jagaimo
potato

洋葱
tamanegi
onion

ピーマン
pīman
sweet pepper

赤唐辛子
aka tōgarashi
chili pepper

ナタウリ
natauri
squash

関連用語 kanrenyōgo ● vocabulary

プチトマト puchi tomato **cherry tomato**	タロ芋 taroimo **taro root**	冷凍 reitō **frozen**	苦い nigai **bitter**	ジャガイモを1キロください。 jagaimo o ichi kiro kudasai. **One kilo of potatoes, please.**
人参 ninjin **carrot**	菱の実 hishi no mi **water chestnut**	生 nama **raw**	硬い katai **firm**	1キロいくらですか。 ichi kiro ikura desuka? **What's the price per kilo?**
新ジャガ shinjaga **new potato**	椎茸 shītake **shitake mushrooms**	辛い karai **hot (spicy)**	果肉 kaniku **flesh**	あれは何と言いますか。 are wa nan to īmasuka? **What are those called?**
セロリアック seroriakku **celeriac**	わさび wasabi **Japanese horseradish**	甘い amai **sweet**	根 ne **root**	

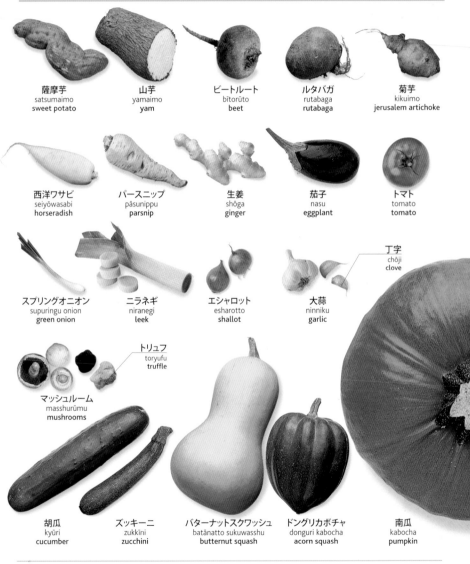

薩摩芋
satsumaimo
sweet potato

山芋
yamaimo
yam

ビートルート
bītorūto
beet

ルタバガ
rutabaga
rutabaga

菊芋
kikuimo
jerusalem artichoke

西洋ワサビ
seiyōwasabi
horseradish

パースニップ
pāsunippu
parsnip

生姜
shōga
ginger

茄子
nasu
eggplant

トマト
tomato
tomato

スプリングオニオン
supuringu onion
green onion

ニラネギ
niranegi
leek

エシャロット
esharotto
shallot

大蒜
ninniku
garlic

丁字
chōji
clove

トリュフ
toryufu
truffle

マッシュルーム
masshurūmu
mushrooms

胡瓜
kyūri
cucumber

ズッキーニ
zukkīni
zucchini

バターナットスクワッシュ
batānatto sukuwasshu
butternut squash

ドングリカボチャ
donguri kabocha
acorn squash

南瓜
kabocha
pumpkin

果物1 kudamono • fruit 1

柑橘類 kankitsu rui • citrus fruit

オレンジ
orenji
orange

クレメンティン
kurementin
clementine

アグリフルーツ
agurifurūtsu
ugli fruit

筋
suji
pith

グレープフルーツ
gurēpufurūtsu
grapefruit

タンジェリン
tanjerin
tangerine

房
fusa
segment

薩摩みかん
satsuma mikan
satsuma

皮
kawa
zest

ライム
raimu
lime

レモン
remon
lemon

金柑
kinkan
kumquat

石果 sekika • stone fruit

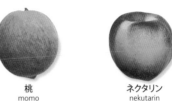

桃
momo
peach

ネクタリン
nekutarin
nectarine

杏
anzu
apricot

プラム
puramu
plum

さくらんぼ
sakurambo
cherry

洋梨
yōnashi
pear

林檎
ringo
apple

果物籠 kudamono kago | basket of fruit

液果とメロン ekika to meron • **berries and melons**

苺
ichigo
strawberry

ラズベリー
razuberī
raspberry

メロン
meron
melon

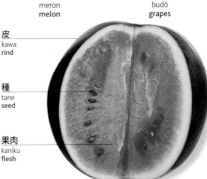
葡萄
budō
grapes

ブラックベリー
burakkuberī
blackberry

レッドカラント
reddokaranto
redcurrant

皮
kawa
rind

種
tane
seed

果肉
kaniku
flesh

クランベリー
kuranberī
cranberry

ブラックカラント
burakkukaranto
blackcurrant

ブルーベリー
burūberī
blueberry

ホワイトカラント
howaitokaranto
whitecurrant

西瓜
suika
watermelon

ローガンベリー
rōganberī
loganberry

グーズベリー
gūzuberī
gooseberry

関連用語 kanrenyōgo • **vocabulary**

ダイオウ daiō rhubarb	酸っぱい suppai sour	パリッとした parittoshita crisp	果汁 kajū juice	熟していますか。 jukushite imasuka? **Are they ripe?**
繊維 sen'i fiber	新鮮 shinsen fresh	腐った kusatta rotten	芯 shin core	試食できますか。 shishoku dekimasuka? **May I try one?**
甘い amai sweet	みずみずしい mizumizushī juicy	(柔らかい)果肉 (yawarakai) kaniku pulp	種なし tanenashi seedless	何日ぐらい保ちますか。 nannichi gurai tamochimasuka? **How long will they keep?**

果物2 kudamono 2 • fruit 2

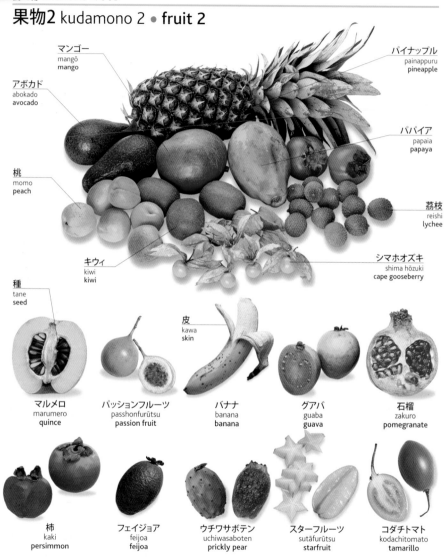

マンゴー
mangō
mango

パイナップル
painappuru
pineapple

アボカド
abokado
avocado

パパイア
papaia
papaya

桃
momo
peach

荔枝
reishi
lychee

キウィ
kiwi
kiwi

シマホオズキ
shima hōzuki
cape gooseberry

種
tane
seed

皮
kawa
skin

マルメロ
marumero
quince

パッションフルーツ
passhonfurūtsu
passion fruit

バナナ
banana
banana

グアバ
guaba
guava

石榴
zakuro
pomegranate

柿
kaki
persimmon

フェイジョア
feijoa
feijoa

ウチワサボテン
uchiwasaboten
prickly pear

スターフルーツ
sutāfurūtsu
starfruit

コダチトマト
kodachitomato
tamarillo

ナッツとドライフルーツ nattsu to doraifurūtsu • nuts and dried fruit

松の実
matsu no mi
pine nut

ピスタチオ
pisutachio
pistachio

カシューナッツ
kashūnattsu
cashew

ピーナッツ
pīnattsu
peanut

ヘーゼルナッツ
hēzerunattsu
hazelnut

ブラジルナッツ
burajirunattsu
brazil nut

ピーカンナッツ
pīkannattsu
pecan

アーモンド
āmondo
almond

胡桃
kurumi
walnut

栗
kuri
chestnut

殻
kara
shell

マカデミアナッツ
makademianattsu
macadamia

無花果
ichijiku
fig

棗
natsume
date

李
sumomo
prune

果肉
kaniku
flesh

サルタナレーズン
sarutana rēzun
seedless raisin

干し葡萄
hoshibudō
raisin

カラント
karanto
currant

ココナッツ
kokonattsu
coconut

関連用語 kanrenyōgo • vocabulary

青い aoi **green**　　硬い katai **hard**　　仁 nin **kernel**　　塩 shio **salted**　　煎った itta **roasted**　　殻を剥いた kara o muita **shelled**　　砂糖漬け果物 satōzuke kudamono **candied fruit**

完熟 kanjuku **ripe**　　柔らかい yawarakai **soft**　　乾燥 kansō **desiccated**　　生 nama **raw**　　季節もの kisetsu mono **seasonal**　　丸ごと marugoto **whole**　　熱帯果実 nettai kajitsu **tropical fruit**

穀類と豆類 kokurui to mamerui • grains and legumes

穀類 kokurui • grains

小麦
komugi
wheat

からす麦
karasumugi
oats

大麦
ōmugi
barley

キビ
kibi
millet

トウモロコシ
tōmorokoshi
corn

キノア
kinoa
quinoa

米 kome • rice

白米
hakumai
white rice

玄米
genmai
brown rice

野生米
yasei mai
wild rice

プディングライス
pudingu raisu
arborio rice

加工穀物 kakō kokumotsu • processed grains

クスクス
kusukusu
couscous

粗挽き麦
arabiki mugi
cracked wheat

セモリナ
semorina
semolina

麸
fusuma
bran

豆類 mamerui ● beans and peas

ライ豆
raimame
butter beans

いんげん豆
ingenmame
navy beans

金時豆
kintoki mame
red kidney beans

小豆
azuki
aduki beans

空豆
soramame
lima beans

大豆
daizu
soybeans

黒目豆
kurome mame
black-eyed beans

鶉豆
uzura mame
pinto beans

緑豆
ryokutō
mung beans

フラジョレ豆
furajore mame
flageolet beans

レンズ豆
renzumame
brown lentils

赤レンティル
aka rentiru
red lentils

グリンピース
gurin pīsu
green peas

雛豆
hiyoko mame
chick peas

スプリットピー
supuritto pī
split peas

種 tane ● seeds

南瓜の種
kabocha no tane
pumpkin seed

辛子の種
karashi no tane
mustard seed

キャラウェイシード
kyarawei shīdo
caraway

胡麻
goma
sesame seed

向日葵の種
himawari no tane
sunflower seed

ハーブと香辛料 hābu to kōshinryō · herbs and spices

香辛料 kōshinryō · spices

バニラ banira | vanilla

ナツメッグ
natsumeggu
nutmeg

メース
mēsu
mace

ウコン
ukon
turmeric

クミン
kumin
cumin

ブーケガルニ
būkegaruni
bouquet garni

オールスパイス
ōrusupaisu
allspice

胡椒の実
koshō no mi
peppercorn

フェヌグリーク
fenugurīku
fenugreek

唐辛子
tōgarashi
chili pepper

丸ごと
marugoto
whole

つぶした
tsubushita
crushed

サフラン
safuran
saffron

カルダモン
karudamon
cardamom

カレー粉
karēko
curry powder

パウダー
paudā
ground

パプリカ
papurika
paprika

フレーク
furēku
flakes

大蒜
ninniku
garlic

ハーブ hābu • herbs

スティック
sutikku
sticks

シナモン
shinamon
cinnamon

レモングラス
remongurasu
lemongrass

クローブ
kurōbu
cloves

大茴香
daiuikyō
star anise

生姜
shōga
ginger

茴香
uikyō
fennel

茴香の種
uikyō no tane
fennel seeds

ローリエ
rōrie
bay leaf

パセリ
paseri
parsley

朝葱
asatsuki
chives

ハッカ
hakka
mint

タイム
taimu
thyme

セージ
sēji
sage

タラゴン
taragon
tarragon

マジョラム
majoramu
marjoram

バジリコ
bajiriko
basil

オレガノ
oregano
oregano

コリアンダー
koriandā
cilantro

ディル
diru
dill

ローズマリー
rōzumarī
rosemary

瓶詰め食品 binzume shokuhin • bottled foods

胡桃油
kurumia bura
walnut oil

コルク栓
koruku sen
cork

向日葵油
himawari abura
sunflower oil

葡萄油
budō abura
grapeseed oil

アーモンドオイル
āmondo oiru
almond oil

胡麻油
goma'abura
sesame seed
oil

ヘーゼルナッツオイル
hēzerunattsu oiru
hazelnut oil

オリーブ油
orībuyu
olive oil

ハーブ
hābu
herbs

香味油
kōmi abura
flavored oil

食用油
shokuyō abura
oils

甘味スプレッド kanmi supureddo • sweet spreads

瓶
bin
jar

ハニカム
hanikamu
honeycomb

クリーム蜂蜜
kurīmu hachimitsu
set honey

レモンカード
remon kādo
lemon curd

ラズベリージャム
razuberī jamu
raspberry jam

マーマレード
māmarēdo
marmalade

透明蜂蜜
tōmei hachimitsu
clear honey

メープルシロップ
mēpuru shiroppu
maple syrup

薬味とスプレッド yakumi to supureddo
• condiments and spreads

林檎酢
ringo su
cider vinegar

バルサミコ酢
barusamiko su
balsamic vinegar

瓶
bin
bottle

イングリッシュマスタード
ingurisshu masutādo
English mustard

マヨネーズ
mayonēzu
mayonnaise

ケチャップ
kechappu
ketchup

ディジョンマスタード
dijon masutādo
French mustard

チャツネ
chatsune
chutney

モルト酢
moruto su
malt vinegar

ワイン酢
wain su
wine vinegar

酢
su
vinegar

ソース
sōsu
sauce

粒マスタード
tsubu masutādo
whole-grain mustard

密封瓶
mippū bin
sealed jar

ピーナッツバター
pīnattsubatā
peanut butter

チョコレートスプレッド
chokorēto supureddo
chocolate spread

瓶詰めフルーツ
binzume furūtsu
preserved fruit

関連用語 kanrenyōgo
• **vocabulary**

コーン油
kōn yu
corn oil

落花生油
rakkasei yu
peanut oil

サラダ油
sarada yu
vegetable oil

菜種油
natane abura
canola oil

コールドプレス油
kōrudopuresu yu
cold-pressed oil

醤油
shōyu
soy sauce

米酢
komezu
rice vinegar

乳製品 nyūseihin • dairy produce

チーズ chīzu • cheese

皮
kawa
rind

粉チーズ
kona chīzu
grated cheese

セミハードチーズ
semihādo chīzu
semihard cheese

ハードチーズ
hādo chīzu
hard cheese

セミソフトチーズ
semisofuto chīzu
semisoft cheese

カッテージチーズ
kattēji chīzu
cottage cheese

クリームチーズ
kurīmu chīzu
cream cheese

生チーズ nama chīzu I fresh cheese

ブルーチーズ
burū chīzu
blue cheese

ソフトチーズ
sofuto chīzu
soft cheese

ミルク miruku • milk

全乳
zennyū
whole milk

低脂肪乳
teishibō-nyū
reduced-fat milk

スキムミルク
sukimu miruku
fat-free milk

牛乳カートン
gyūnyū kāton
milk carton

牛乳 gyūnyū I cow's milk

山羊乳
yagi-nyū
goat's milk

練乳
rennyū
condensed milk

バター
batā
butter

マーガリン
māgarin
margarine

生クリーム
nama kuriīmu
cream

シングルクリーム
shinguru kurīmu
light cream

ダブルクリーム
daburu kurīmu
double cream

ホイップクリーム
hoippu kurīmu
whipped cream

サワークリーム
sawā kurīmu
sour cream

ヨーグルト
yōguruto
yogurt

アイスクリーム
aisukurīmu
ice cream

卵 tamago • eggs

卵黄
ran'ō
yolk

卵白
rampaku
egg white

殻
kara
shell

エッグカップ
eggu kappu
egg cup

ゆで卵 yudetamago I boiled egg

鵞鳥の卵
gachō no tamago
goose egg

鶏卵
keiran
hen's egg

鶉卵
uzura tamago
quail egg

家鴨の卵
ahiru no tamago
duck egg

関連用語 kanrenyōgo • vocabulary

低温殺菌
teionsakkin
pasteurized

ミルクセーキ
mirukusēki
milkshake

塩入り
shio-iri
salted

羊乳
yōnyū
sheep's milk

乳糖
nyūtō
lactose

ホモジナイズ
homojinaizu
homogenized

低温殺菌していない
teionsakkin shiteinai
unpasteurized

フローズンヨーグルト
furōzun yōguruto
frozen yogurt

無塩
muen
unsalted

バターミルク
batāmiruku
buttermilk

無脂肪
mu-shibō
fat-free

粉乳
funnyū
powdered milk

パンと小麦粉 pan to komugiko • **breads and flours**

スライス食パン
suraisu shokupan
sliced bread

ケシの実
keshi no mi
poppy seeds

ライ麦パン
raimugi pan
rye bread

バゲット
bagetto
baguette

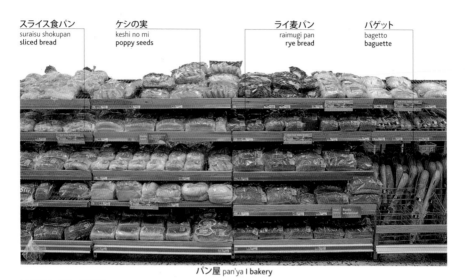

パン屋 pan'ya I **bakery**

パン作り pan-zukuri • **making bread**

白小麦粉
shiro komugiko
white flour

黒小麦粉
kuro komugiko
brown flour

全粒粉
zenryū-fun
whole-wheat flour

酵母
kōbo
yeast

篩にかける furui ni kakeru
sift (v)

パン生地
pan kiji
dough

混ぜる mazeru I **mix (v)**

こねる koneru I **knead (v)**

焼く yaku I **bake (v)**

耳
mimi
crust

食パンの塊
shokupan no
katamari
loaf

スライス
suraisu
slice

白パン
shiro pan
white bread

黒パン
kuro pan
brown bread

全粒パン
zenryū pan
whole-wheat bread

グラナリブレッド
guranari bureddo
multigrain bread

とうもろこしパン
tōmorokoshi pan
cornbread

ソーダパン
sōda pan
soda bread

サワードウブレッド
sawādo-u bureddo
sourdough bread

フラットブレッド
furattobureddo
flatbread

ベーグル
bēguru
bagel

バップ
bappu | **bun**

ロールパン
rōrupan | **roll**

フルーツパン
furūtsu pan
fruit bread

種入りパン
tane-iri pan
seeded bread

ナン
nan
naan bread

ピタパン
pita pan
pita bread

クリスプブレッド
kurisupu bureddo
crispbread

関連用語 kanrenyōgo • vocabulary

強力粉 kyōrikiko **bread flour**	**膨れる** fukureru **rise (v)**	**発酵させる** hakkō saseru **prove (v)**	**パン粉** panko **breadcrumbs**	**スライサー** suraisā **slicer**
膨らし粉入り小麦粉 fukurashiko-iri komugiko **self-raising flour**	**薄力粉** hakurikiko **all-purpose flour**	**グレーズを塗る** gurēzu o nuru **glaze (v)**	**波形** namigata **flute**	**パン職人** pan shokunin **baker**

ケーキとデザート kēki to dezāto • cakes and desserts

エクレア
ekurea
éclair

シュー皮
shū-gawa
choux pastry

パイ生地
pai kiji
puff pastry

クリーム
kurīmu
cream

フィロペストリー
firo pesutorī
phyllo pastry

具
gu
filling

チョコレートを被せた
chokorēto o kabuseta
chocolate-coated

フルーツケーキ
furūtsu kēki
fruit cake

マフィン
mafin
muffin

フルーツタルト
furūtsu taruto
fruit tart

メランゲ
merange
meringue

スポンジケーキ
suponji kēki
sponge cake

ケーキ kēki I cakes

関連用語 kanrenyōgo • vocabulary

カスタードクリーム kasutādo kurīmu crème pâtissière	丸い小型パン marui kogata pan bun	ペストリー pesutorī pastry	ライスプディング raisu pudingu rice pudding	一切れください。 hitokire kudasai? May I have a slice please?
チョコレートケーキ chokorēto kēki chocolate cake	カスタード kasutādo custard	一切れ hitokire slice	お祝い oiwai celebration	

チョコレートチップス
chokorēto chippusu
chocolate chip

スポンジフィンガー
suponji fingā
lady finger

フロレンティン
furorentin
florentine

トライフル
toraifuru
trifle

ビスケット bisuketto I **biscuits**

ムース
mūsu
mousse

シャーベット
shābetto
sorbet

クリームパイ
kurīmu pai
cream pie

プリン
purin
crème caramel

お祝い用ケーキ oiwai-yō kēki • celebration cakes

最上段
saijōdan
top tier

リボン
ribon
ribbon

下段
gedan
bottom tier

アイシング
aishingu
icing

マジパン
majipan
marzipan

ウェディングケーキ wedingu kēki
wedding cake

飾り
kazari
decoration

誕生日ケーキの蝋燭
tanjōbi kēki no rōsoku
birthday candles

吹き消す
fukikesu
blow out (v)

誕生日ケーキ tanjōbi kēki I **birthday cake**

デリカテッセン derikatessen ● delicatessen

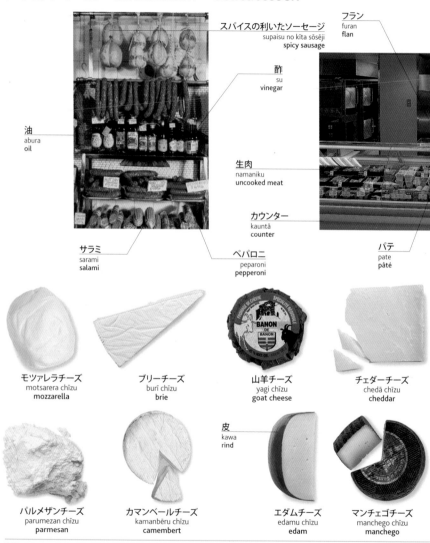

スパイスの利いたソーセージ
supaisu no kīta sōsēji
spicy sausage

フラン
furan
flan

酢
su
vinegar

油
abura
oil

生肉
namaniku
uncooked meat

カウンター
kauntā
counter

サラミ
sarami
salami

ペパロニ
peparoni
pepperoni

パテ
pate
pâté

モツァレラチーズ
motsarera chīzu
mozzarella

ブリーチーズ
burī chīzu
brie

山羊チーズ
yagi chīzu
goat cheese

チェダーチーズ
chedā chīzu
cheddar

パルメザンチーズ
parumezan chīzu
parmesan

カマンベールチーズ
kamanbēru chīzu
camembert

皮
kawa
rind

エダムチーズ
edamu chīzu
edam

マンチェゴチーズ
manchego chīzu
manchego

パイ
pai
potpies

黒オリーブ
kuro orību
black olive

唐辛子
tōgarashi
chili

ソース
sōsu
sauce

ロールパン
rōrupan
bread roll

調理肉
chōri niku
cooked meat

緑オリーブ
midori orību
green olive

ハム
hamu
ham

サンドイッチ売場 sandoitchi uriba | **sandwich counter**

魚の薫製
sakana no kunsei
smoked fish

ケーパー
kēpā
capers

チョリソ
choriso
chorizo

プロシュット
puroshutto
prosciutto

スタッフドオリーブ
sutaffudo orību
stuffed olive

関連用語 kanrenyōgo • vocabulary

油漬け abura-zuke **in oil**	マリネ marine **marinated**	薫製 kunsei **smoked**
塩水漬け shiomizu-zuke **in brine**	塩漬け shiozuke **salted**	保存処理 hozon shori **cured**

番号札を取ってください。
bangō fuda o totte kudasai.
Take a number please.

それを試食できますか。
sore o shishoku dekimasuka?
May I try some of that please?

それを6切れください。
sore o rokkire kudasai.
Six slices of that, please

飲物 nomimono • drinks

水 mizu • water

容器入り飲料水
yōki-iri inryōsui
bottled water

発泡
happō
sparkling

スティル
sutiru
still

水道水
suidōsui
tap water

トニックウォーター
tonikku wōtā
tonic water

ソーダ水
sōdasui
soda water

ミネラルウォーター mineraru wōtā
mineral water

暖かい飲物 atatakai nomimono • hot drinks

ティーバッグ
tī baggu
teabag

リーフティー
rīfu tī
loose leaf tea

紅茶
kōcha
tea

コーヒー豆
kōhī-mame
beans

コーヒー粉
kōhī-fun
ground coffee

コーヒー
kōhī
coffee

ホットココア
hotto kokoa
hot chocolate

麦芽飲料
bakuga inryō
malted drink

ソフトドリンク sofuto dorinku • soft drinks

ストロー
sutorō
straw

トマトジュース
tomato jūsu
tomato juice

グレープジュース
gurēpu jūsu
grape juice

レモネード
remonēdo
lemonade

オレンジエード
orenjiēdo
orangeade

コーラ
kōra
cola

アルコール飲料 arukōru inryō ● alcoholic drinks

ジン
jin | gin

ビール
bīru
beer

缶
kan
can

林檎酒
ringoshu
hard cider

ビター
bitā
bitter

黒ビール
kurobīru
stout

ウォッカ
wokka | vodka

ウイスキー uisukī | whisky

ラム酒
ramushu
rum

ブランデー
burandē
brandy

ポートワイン
pōtowain
port

シェリー
sherī
sherry

辛口
karakuchi
dry

カンパリ
kampari
campari

ロゼ（ワイン）
roze (wain)
rosé (wine)

白（ワイン）
shiro (wain)
white (wine)

赤（ワイン）
aka (wain)
red (wine)

リキュール
rikyūru
liqueur

テキーラ
tekīra
tequila

シャンパン
shampan
champagne

ワイン wain | wine

外食 gaishoku
eating out

カフェ kafe · **café**

パラソル
parasoru
umbrella

オーニング
ōningu
awning

メニュー
menyū
menu

テラスカフェ
terasu kafe
terrace café

ウェイター
weitā
waiter

コーヒーメーカー
kōhī mēkā
coffee machine

テーブル
tēburu
table

路上カフェ rojō kafe | **pavement café**

スナックバー sunakku bā | **snack bar**

コーヒー kōhī · **coffee**

ミルクコーヒー
miruku kōhī
white coffee

ブラックコーヒー
burak kukōhī
black coffee

ココアパウダー
kokoa paudā
cocoa powder

泡
awa
froth

フィルターコーヒー
firutā kōhī
filter coffee

エスプレッソ
esupuresso
espresso

カプチーノ
kapuchīno
cappuccino

アイスコーヒー
aisu kōhī
iced coffee

紅茶 kōcha • tea

ハーブ茶
hābu cha
herbal tea

カモミール茶
kamomīru cha
camomile tea

緑茶
ryokucha
green tea

ミルクティー
miruku tī
tea with milk

紅茶
kōcha
black tea

レモンティー
remon tī
tea with lemon

ミントティー
minto tī
mint tea

アイスティー
aisu tī
iced tea

ジュースとミルクセーキ jūsu to mirukusēki • juices and milkshakes

チョコレートミルクセーキ
chokorēto mirukusēki
chocolate milkshake

苺のミルクセーキ
ichigo no mirukusēki
strawberry milkshake

コーヒーミルクセーキ
kōhī mirukusēki
coffee milkshake

オレンジジュース
orenji jūsu
orange juice

林檎ジュース
ringo jūsu
apple juice

パイナップルジュース
painappuru jūsu
pineapple juice

トマトジュース
tomato jūsu
tomato juice

食べ物 tabemono • food

スクープ
sukūpu
scoop

黒パン
kuro pan
brown bread

トーストサンド
tōsuto-sando
toasted sandwich

サラダ
sarada
salad

アイスクリーム
aisukurīmu
ice cream

ペストリー
pesutorī
pastry

バー bā • bar

グラス
gurasu
glasses

計量器
keiryōki
dispenser

レジ
reji
cash register

バーテン
bāten
bartender

タップ
tappu
beer tap

コーヒーメーカー
kōhī mēkā
coffee machine

アイスバケツ
aisu baketsu
ice bucket

バースツール
bā sutsūru
bar stool

灰皿
haizara
ashtray

コースター
kōsutā
coaster

カウンター
kauntā
bar counter

栓抜き
sennuki
bottle opener

氷ばさみ
kōri-basami
tongs

マドラー
madorā
stirrer

レバー
rebā
lever

メジャーカップ
mejā kappu
measure

コルク栓抜き koruku sennuki **I corkscrew**

シェーカー shēkā
cocktail shaker

水差し
mizusashi
pitcher

角氷
kaku-gōri
ice cube

ジントニック
jintonikku
gin and tonic

スコッチの水割り
sukotchi no mizuwari
scotch and water

キューバリブレ
kyūba ribure
rum and coke

スクリュードライバー
sukuryū doraibā
vodka and orange

マティーニ
matīni
martini

カクテル
kakuteru
cocktail

ワイン
wain
wine

ビール bīru I beer

ダブル
daburu
double

シングル
shinguru
single

氷とレモン
kōri to remon
ice and lemon

ワンショット
wanshotto
a shot

分量
bunryō
measure

氷無し
kōri nashi
without ice

氷入り
kōri-iri
with ice

お摘み o-tsumami • bar snacks

カシューナッツ
kashūnattsu
cashew nuts

ピーナッツ
pīnattsu
peanuts

アーモンド
āmondo
almonds

ポテトチップス poteto chippusu
potato chips

ナッツ nattsu I nuts

オリーブ orību I olives

レストラン resutoran • restaurant

禁煙席
kin'en seki
nonsmoking section

ナプキン
napukin
napkin

コミシェフ
komi shefu
commis chef

テーブルセッティング
tēburu settingu
table setting

シェフ
shefu
chef

グラス
gurasu
glass

トレイ
torei
tray

キッチン kitchin | kitchen

ウェイター weitā | waiter

関連用語 kanrenyōgo • vocabulary

ワインリスト wain risuto **wine list**	**デザートワゴン** dezāto wagon **dessert cart**	**領収書** ryōshūsho **receipt**	**サービス料抜き** sābisu-ryō nuki **service not included**	**喫煙席** kitsuen seki **smoking section**	**胡椒** koshō **pepper**
酒 sake **rice wine**	**値段** nedan **price**	**チップ** chippu **tip**	**ビュッフェ** byuffe **buffet**	**客** kyaku **customer**	**座卓** zataku **(low Japanese) table**
アラカルト arakaruto **à la carte**	**会計** kaikei **check**	**サービス料込み** sābisu-ryō komi **service included**	**お薦め料理** o-susume ryōri **specials**	**塩** shio **salt**	**座布団** zabuton **(Japanese) cushion**

メニュー
menyū
menu

お子様メニュー
okosama menyū
child's meal

注文する chūmon suru | **order (v)**

支払う shiharau | **pay (v)**

コース料理 kōsu ryōri • courses

食前酒
shokuzenshu
aperitif

前菜
zensai
appetizer

スープ
sūpu
soup

主菜
shusai
main course

サイドオーダー
saido ōdā
side order

フォーク
fōku
fork

コーヒースプーン
kōhī supūn
coffee spoon

デザート dezāto
dessert

コーヒー kōhī | **coffee**

2人分の席をお願いします。
futari-bun no seki o onegaishimasu.
A table for two please.

メニュー/ワインリストを見せてください。
menyū/wainrisuto o misete kudasai?
May I see the menu/winelist please?

セットメニューはありますか。
setto menyū wa arimasuka?
Is there a fixed price menu?

ベジタリアン料理はありますか。
bejitarian ryōri wa arimasuka?
Do you have any vegetarian dishes?

会計/領収書をお願いします。
o-kaikei/ryōshūsho o onegaishimasu?
Could I have the check/a receipt please?

会計は別々にお願いします。
kaikei wa betsubetsu ni onegaishimasu?
Can we pay separately?

お手洗いはどこですか。
o-tearai wa doko desuka?
Where are the restrooms, please?

ファーストフード fāsuto fūdo・**fast food**

ストロー
sutorō
straw

ハンバーガー
hambāgā
burger

ソフトドリンク
sofuto dorinku
soft drink

フライドポテト
furaido poteto
french fries

ペーパーナプキン
pēpā napukin
paper napkin

トレイ
torei
tray

バーガーミール bāgā mīru | burger meal

ピザ
piza
pizza

価格表
kakaku hyō
price list

缶飲料
kan inryō
canned drink

宅配 takuhai | **home delivery**

露店 roten | **street stand**

関連用語 kanrenyōgo・vocabulary

ピザ屋
piza-ya
pizza parlor

ハンバーガー屋
hambāgā-ya
burger bar

メニュー
menyū
menu

店内飲食
tennai inshoku
eat-in

持ち帰り
mochikaeri
takeout

温め直す
atatamenaosu
reheat (v)

ケチャップ
ketchappu
ketchup

おにぎり
onigiri
rice ball

弁当
bentō
lunch box

それを持ち帰りにしてください。
sore o mochikaeri ni shite kudasai?
Can I have that to go, please?

出前はできますか。
demae wa dekimasuka?
Do you deliver?

バンズ
banzu
bun

マスタード
masutādo
mustard

ソーセージ
sōsēji
sausage

ハンバーガー
hambāgā
hamburger

チキンバーガー
chikin bāgā
chicken burger

ベジバーガー
beji bāgā
veggie burger

ホットドッグ hotto doggu
hot dog

具
gu
filling

サンドイッチ
sandoitchi
sandwich

クラブサンド
kurabu-sando
club sandwich

オープンサンド
ōpun-sando
open-face sandwich

ラップサンド
rappu-sando
wrap

ソース
sōsu
sauce

塩味
shioaji
savory

甘い
amai
sweet

トッピング
toppingu
topping

ケバブ
kebabu
kebab

チキンナゲット
chikin nagetto
chicken nuggets

クレープ kurēpu | crêpes

フィッシュ＆チップス
fisshu ando chippusu
fish and chips

スペアリブ
supea ribu
ribs

フライドチキン
furaido chikin
fried chicken

ピザ
piza
pizza

朝食 chōshoku • breakfast

牛乳
gyūnyū
milk

シリアル
shiriaru
cereal

ジャム
jamu
jam

ドライフルーツ
dorai furūtsu
dried fruit

ハム
hamu
ham

チーズ
chīzu
cheese

クリスプブレッド
kurisupu bureddo
crispbread

朝食ビュッフェ
chōshoku byuffe
breakfast buffet

マーマレード
māmarēdo
marmalade

パテ
pate
pâté

バター
batā
butter

果物ジュース
kudamono jūsu
fruit juice

コーヒー
kōhī
coffee

ホットココア
hotto kokoa
hot chocolate

クロワッサン
kurowassan
croissant

紅茶
kōcha
tea

朝食のテーブル chōshoku no tēburu | breakfast table

飲物 nomimono | drinks

トマト
tomato
tomato

ブラックプディング
burakku pudingu
black pudding

トースト
tōsuto
toast

目玉焼き
medamayaki
fried egg

ソーセージ
sōsēji
sausage

ベーコン
bēkon
bacon

ブリオッシュ
buriosshu
brioche

パン
pan
bread

イングリッシュ・ブレックファースト
ingurisshu burekkufāsuto
English breakfast

黄身
kimi
yolk

薫製ニシン
kunsei nishin
kippers

フレンチトースト
furenchi tōsuto
french toast

ゆで卵
yudetamago
boiled egg

スクランブルエッグ
sukuramburu eggu
scrambled eggs

クリーム
kurīmu
cream

フルーツヨーグルト
furūtsu yōguruto
fruit yogurt

パンケーキ
pankēki
pancakes

ワッフル
waffuru
waffles

ポリッジ
porijji
oatmeal

フルーツサラダ
furūtsu sarada
fruit salad

食事 shokuji • dinner

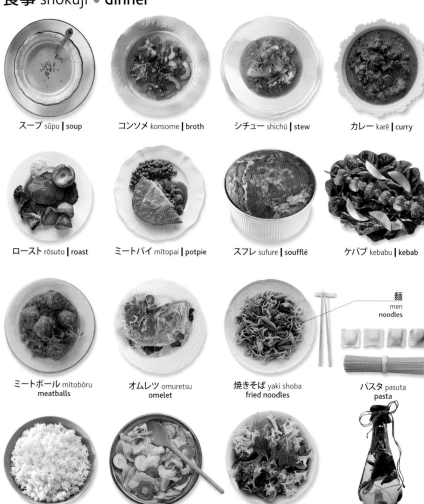

スープ sūpu | soup

コンソメ konsome | broth

シチュー shichū | stew

カレー karē | curry

ロースト rōsuto | roast

ミートパイ mītopai | potpie

スフレ sufure | soufflé

ケバブ kebabu | kebab

麺
men
noodles

ミートボール mītobōru
meatballs

オムレツ omuretsu
omelet

焼きそば yaki shoba
fried noodles

パスタ pasuta
pasta

ご飯 gohan | rice

ミックスサラダ mikkusu sarada
tossed salad

グリーンサラダ gurīn sarada
green salad

サラダドレッシング sarada
doresshingu | dressing

調理方法 chōri hōhō • techniques

詰め物 tsumemono
stuffed

煮込んだ nikonda | **in sauce**

（グリルで）焼いた
(guriru de) yaita | **grilled**

マリネ marine | **marinated**

（沸騰前の温度で）茹でた (futtō
mae no ondo de) yudeta | **poached**

つぶした tsubushita
mashed

（オーブンで）焼いた
(ōbun de) yaita | **baked**

（フライパンで）焼いた
(furaipan de) yaita | **pan-fried**

炒めた itameta | **fried**

ピクルス pikurusu | **pickled**

薫製 kunsei | **smoked**

揚げた ageta | **deep-fried**

シロップ漬け shiroppu-zuke
in syrup

ドレッシングをかけた
doresshingu o kaketa | **dressed**

蒸した mushita | **steamed**

保存処理した
hozon shori shita | **cured**

学習 gakushū
study

学校 gakkō • school

先生
sensei
teacher

黒板
kokuban
blackboard

男子生徒 danshi seito
schoolboy

生徒
seito
pupil

学校の制服
gakkō no seifuku
school uniform

机
tsukue
desk

通学鞄
tsūgaku kaban
school bag

チョーク
chōku
chalk

教室 kyōshitsu | classroom

女子生徒
joshi seito
schoolgirl

関連用語 kanrenyōgo • vocabulary

歴史 rekishi history	科学 kagaku science	物理 butsuri physics
外国語 gaikokugo languages	美術 bijutsu art	化学 kagaku chemistry
文学 bungaku literature	音楽 ongaku music	生物 seibutsu biology
地理 chiri geography	数学 sūgaku math	体育 tai'iku physical education

学業 gakugyō • activities

読む yomu | read (v)

書く kaku | write (v)

綴る tsuzuru | spell (v)

描く egaku | draw (v)

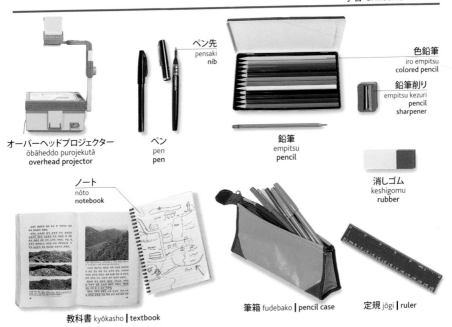

オーバーヘッドプロジェクター
ōbāheddo purojekutā
overhead projector

ペン
pen
pen

ペン先
pensaki
nib

色鉛筆
iro empitsu
colored pencil

鉛筆削り
empitsu kezuri
pencil sharpener

鉛筆
empitsu
pencil

消しゴム
keshigomu
rubber

ノート
nōto
notebook

教科書 kyōkasho | **textbook**

筆箱 fudebako | **pencil case**

定規 jōgi | **ruler**

質問する shitsumon suru
question (v)

答える kotaeru | **answer (v)**

話し合う hanashiau | **discuss (v)**

学ぶ manabu | **learn (v)**

関連用語 kanrenyōgo • vocabulary

校長先生 kōchō sensei **principal**	答え kotae **answer**	成績 seiseki **grade**
授業 jugyō **lesson**	宿題 shukudai **homework**	学年 gakunen **year**
質問 shitsumon **question**	試験 shiken **test**	辞書 jisho **dictionary**
ノートを取る nōto o toru **take notes (v)**	作文 sakubun **essay**	百科事典 hyakkajiten **encyclopedia**

数学 sūgaku • math

平面図形 heimenzukei • shapes

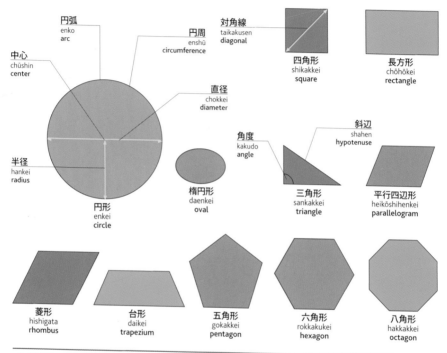

円弧
enko
arc

円周
enshū
circumference

中心
chūshin
center

直径
chokkei
diameter

半径
hankei
radius

円形
enkei
circle

楕円形
daenkei
oval

対角線
taikakusen
diagonal

四角形
shikakkei
square

長方形
chōhōkei
rectangle

角度
kakudo
angle

斜辺
shahen
hypotenuse

三角形
sankakkei
triangle

平行四辺形
heikōshihenkei
parallelogram

菱形
hishigata
rhombus

台形
daikei
trapezium

五角形
gokakkei
pentagon

六角形
rokkakukei
hexagon

八角形
hakkakkei
octagon

立体図形 rittaizukei • solids

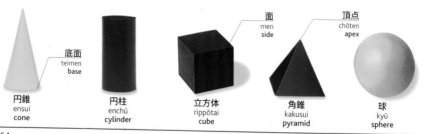

面
men
side

頂点
chōten
apex

底面
teimen
base

円錐
ensui
cone

円柱
enchū
cylinder

立方体
rippōtai
cube

角錐
kakusui
pyramid

球
kyū
sphere

線 sen • lines

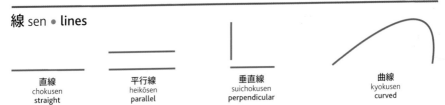

直線	平行線	垂直線	曲線
chokusen	heikōsen	suichokusen	kyokusen
straight	parallel	perpendicular	curved

測定 sokutei • measurements

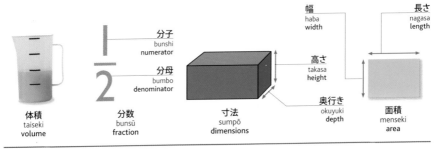

幅
haba
width

長さ
nagasa
length

分子
bunshi
numerator

分母
bumbo
denominator

高さ
takasa
height

奥行き
okuyuki
depth

体積
taiseki
volume

分数
bunsū
fraction

寸法
sumpō
dimensions

面積
menseki
area

数学用品 sūgaku yōhin • equipment

三角定規
sankakujōgi
set square

分度器
bundoki
protractor

定規
jōgi
ruler

コンパス
kompasu
compass

電卓
dentaku
calculator

関連用語 kanrenyōgo • vocabulary

幾何学	プラス	掛ける	イコール	足す	掛ける	数式
kikagaku	purasu	kakeru	ikōru	tasu	kakeru	sūshiki
geometry	plus	times	equals	add (v)	multiply (v)	equation

算数	マイナス	割る	数える	引く	割る	百分率
sansū	mainasu	waru	kazoeru	hiku	waru	hyakubunritsu
arithmetic	minus	divided by	count (v)	subtract (v)	divide (v)	percentage

科学 kagaku • science

坩堝
rutsubo
crucible

重り
omori
weight

ブンゼンバーナー
bunzen bānā
bunsen burner

実験室
jikken shitsu
laboratory

天秤
tembin
scale

バネ秤
banebakari
spring balance

三脚
sankyaku
tripod

スタンド
sutando
clamp stand

ガラス瓶
garasu bin
glass bottle

試験管
shikenkan
test tube

試験管立て
shikenkan-tate
rack

漏斗
rōto
funnel

クランプ
kurampu
clamp

ストッパー
sutoppā
stopper

タイマー
taimā
timer

フラスコ
furasuko
flask

シャーレー
shārē
petri dish

実験 jikken | experiment

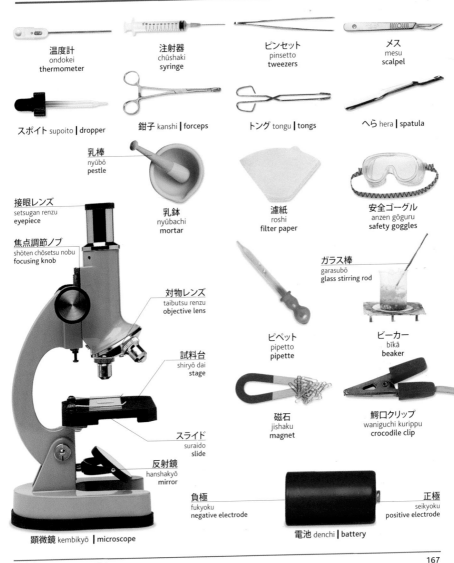

温度計
ondokei
thermometer

注射器
chūshaki
syringe

ピンセット
pinsetto
tweezers

メス
mesu
scalpel

スポイト supoito | dropper

鉗子 kanshi | forceps

トング tongu | tongs

へら hera | spatula

乳棒
nyūbō
pestle

乳鉢
nyūbachi
mortar

濾紙
roshi
filter paper

安全ゴーグル
anzen gōguru
safety goggles

接眼レンズ
setsugan renzu
eyepiece

焦点調節ノブ
shōten chōsetsu nobu
focusing knob

対物レンズ
taibutsu renzu
objective lens

試料台
shiryō dai
stage

スライド
suraido
slide

反射鏡
hanshakyō
mirror

ガラス棒
garasubō
glass stirring rod

ピペット
pipetto
pipette

ビーカー
bīkā
beaker

磁石
jishaku
magnet

鰐口クリップ
waniguchi kurippu
crocodile clip

負極
fukyoku
negative electrode

正極
seikyoku
positive electrode

顕微鏡 kembikyō | microscope

電池 denchi | battery

大学 daigaku • college

スポーツフィールド
supōtsu firudo
playing field

入学事務局
nyūgaku
jimukyoku
admissions

学生食堂
gakusei shokudō
refectory

学生寮
gakusei ryō
residence hall

医療センター
iryō sentā
health center

キャンパス kyampasu | campus

図書目録
tosho mokuroku
card catalog

関連用語 kanrenyōgo • vocabulary

図書カード tosho kādo **library card**	問い合わせ toiawase **help desk**	借出し karidashi **loan**
閲覧室 etsuran shitsu **reading room**	借りる kariru **borrow (v)**	本 hon **book**
読書リスト dokusho risuto **reading list**	予約する yoyaku suru **reserve (v)**	題名 daimei **title**
返却日 henkyaku-bi **return date**	延長する enchō suru **renew (v)**	通路 tsūro **aisle**

司書
shisho
librarian

貸出カウンター
kashidashi kauntā
circulation desk

書架
shoka
bookshelf

定期刊行物
teiki kankōbutsu
periodical

雑誌
zasshi
journal

図書館 toshokan | library

大学生 daigakusei undergraduate

講師 kôshi lecturer

卒業生 sotsugyôsei graduate

ローブ rôbu robe

講堂 kôdô | lecture hall

卒業式 sotsugyô-shiki | graduation ceremony

専門学校 senmongakkō • schools

モデル moderu model

美術大学 bijutsu daigaku
art college

音楽学校 ongaku gakkō
music school

舞踊学院 buyō gakuin
dance academy

関連用語 kanrenyōgo • vocabulary

奨学金 shōgakuhin scholarship	**研究** kenkyū research	**学位論文** gakui-rombun dissertation	**医学** igaku medicine	**哲学** tetsugaku philosophy
卒業証書 sotsugyō-shōsho diploma	**修士号** shūshi gō master's	**学部** gakubu department	**動物学** dōbutsugaku zoology	**文学** bungaku literature
学位 gakui degree	**博士号** hakase gō doctorate	**法学** hōgaku law	**物理学** butsurigaku physics	**美術史** bijutsushi art history
大学院 daigakuin postgraduate	**卒業論文** sotsugyō-rombun thesis	**工学** kōgaku engineering	**政治学** seijigaku politics	**経済学** keizaigaku economics

仕事 shigoto
work

事務所1 jimusho • office 1

事務所 jimusho • office

モニター
monitā
monitor

デスクトップオーガナイザー
desukutoppu ōganaizā
desktop organizer

ファイル
fairu
file

未決済箱
mikessai-bako
in-tray

決済箱
kessai-bako
out-tray

パソコン
pasokon
computer

キーボード
kībōdo
keyboard

電話
denwa
telephone

ノート
nōto
notebook

ラベル
raberu
label

机
tsukue
desk

ゴミ箱
gomibako
wastebasket

回転椅子
kaiten isu
swivel chair

ワゴン
wagon
drawer unit

引出し
hikidashi
drawer

ファイリングキャビネット
fairingu kyabinetto
filing cabinet

事務機器 jimu kiki • office equipment

給紙トレイ
kyūshi torei
paper tray

用紙ガイド
yōshi gaido
paper guide

ファックス
fakkusu
fax

プリンタ purinta | **printer**

ファックス fakkusu | **fax machine**

関連用語 kanrenyōgo • vocabulary

印刷する
insatsu suru
print (v)

拡大する
kakudai suru
enlarge (v)

複写する
fukusha suru
copy (v)

縮小する
shukushō suru
reduce (v)

コピーを取らなければなりません。
kopī o toranakereba narimasen.
I need to make some copies.

事務用品 jimu yōhin • office supplies

謹呈スリップ
kintei surippu
notecard

レターヘッド
retāheddo
letterhead

封筒
fūtō
envelope

箱型ファイル
hako-gata fairu
file box

インデックス
indekkusu
tab

仕切りカード
shikiri kādo
divider

クリップボード
kurippubōdo
clipboard

ノート
nōto
notepad

吊り下げ式フォルダー
tsurisage-shiki forudā
hanging file

ドキュメントファイル
dokyumento fairu
accordion file

レバーアーチ式ファイル
rebā'āchi-shiki fairu
binder

(ホチキスの)針
(hochikisu no) shin
staples

セロテープ
serotēpu
sticky tape

スタンプ台
sutampu dai
ink pad

システム手帳
shisutemu techō
personal organizer

ホチキス
hochikisu
stapler

テープカッター
tēpu kattā
tape dispenser

穴あけパンチ
ana'ake panchi
hole punch

ゴム印
gomuin
rubber stamp

輪ゴム
wagomu
rubber band

目玉クリップ
medama kurippu
bulldog clip

ゼムクリップ
zemu kurippu
paper clip

画鋲
gabyō
push pin

掲示板 keijiban | **bulletin board**

事務所2 jimusho • office 2

フリップチャート
furippu chāto
flipchart

イーゼル
īzeru
easel

マネージャー
manējā
manager

提案書
teian sho
proposal

報告書
hōkokusho
report

幹部
kambu
executive

議事録
gijiroku
minutes

会議 kaigi | meeting

関連用語 kanrenyōgo • vocabulary

会議室
kaigi shitsu
meeting room

出席する
shusseki suru
attend (v)

議題
gidai
agenda

議長を務める
gichō o tsutomeru
chair (v)

会議は何時ですか。
kaigi wa nanji desuka?
What time is the meeting?

営業時間は何時から何時までですか。
eigyōjikan wa nanji kara nanji made desuka?
What are your office hours?

プレゼンター
purezentā
speaker

プロジェクター
purojekutā
projector

プレゼンテーション purezentēshon | presentation

ビジネス bijinesu · business

ノートパソコン
nōtopasokon
laptop

メモ
memo
notes

ビジネスマン
bijinesuman
businessman

ビジネスウーマン
bijimesu'ūman
businesswoman

ビジネスランチ bijinesu ranchi | business lunch

出張 shutchō | business trip

手帳 techō | diary

取引先
torihikisaki
client

予定
yotei
appointment

電子手帳
denshitechō
electronic diary

社長
shachō
CEO

商取引 shōtorihiki | business deal

関連用語 kanrenyōgo · vocabulary

会社
kaisha
company

従業員
jūgyōin
staff

経理部
keiri bu
accounts department

法務部
hōmu bu
legal department

本社
honsha
headquarters

給料
kyūryō
salary

市場開発部
shijōkaihatsu bu
marketing department

顧客サービス部
kokyaku sābisu bu
customer service department

支社
shisha
regional office

従業員名簿
jūgyōin meibo
payroll

営業部
eigyō bu
sales department

人事部
jinji bu
human resources department

コンピュータ kompyūta・**computer**

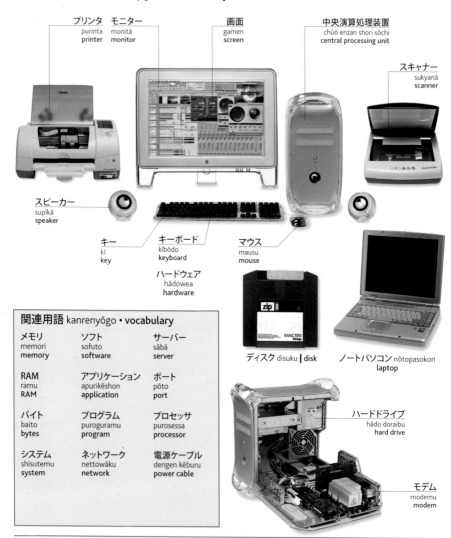

プリンタ
purinta
printer

モニター
monitā
monitor

画面
gamen
screen

中央演算処理装置
chūō enzan shori sōchi
central processing unit

スキャナー
sukyanā
scanner

スピーカー
supīkā
speaker

キー
kī
key

キーボード
kībōdo
keyboard

マウス
mausu
mouse

ハードウェア
hādowea
hardware

ディスク disuku | **disk**

ノートパソコン nōtopasokon
laptop

ハードドライブ
hādo doraibu
hard drive

モデム
modemu
modem

関連用語 kanrenyōgo・**vocabulary**

メモリ
memori
memory

ソフト
sofuto
software

サーバー
sābā
server

RAM
ramu
RAM

アプリケーション
apurikēshon
application

ポート
pōto
port

バイト
baito
bytes

プログラム
puroguramu
program

プロセッサ
purosessa
processor

システム
shisutemu
system

ネットワーク
nettowāku
network

電源ケーブル
dengen kēburu
power cable

デスクトップ desukutoppu · desktop

ファイル
fairu
file

フォルダ
foruda
folder

ごみ箱
gomibako
trash

メニューバー
menyūbā
menubar

ツールバー
tsūrubā
toolbar

壁紙
kabegami
wallpaper

フォント
fonto
font

アイコン
aikon
icon

スクロールバー
sukurōrubā
scrollbar

ウィンドウ
windo-u
window

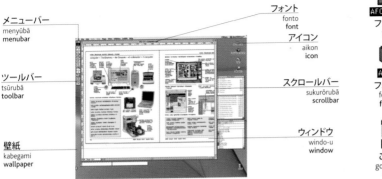

インターネット intānetto · internet

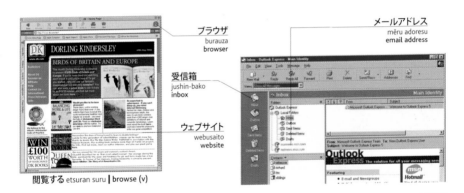

ブラウザ
burauza
browser

受信箱
jushin-bako
inbox

ウェブサイト
webusaito
website

閲覧する etsuran suru | browse (v)

電子メール denshimēru · email

メールアドレス
mēru adoresu
email address

関連用語 kanrenyōgo · vocabulary

接続する
setsuzoku suru
connect (v)

サービスプロバイダ
sābisu purobaida
service provider

ログオンする
roguon suru
log on (v)

ダウンロードする
daunrōdo suru
download (v)

送信する
sōshin suru
send (v)

保存する
hozon suru
save (v)

インストールする
insutōru suru
install (v)

メールアカウント
mēru akaunto
email account

オンライン
onrain
online

添付書類
tempu shorui
attachment

受信する
jushin suru
receive (v)

検索する
kensaku suru
search (v)

報道 hōdō • media

テレビスタジオ terebi sutajio • television studio

司会者
shikai-sha
presenter

照明
shōmei
light

セット
setto
set

カメラ
kamera
camera

カメラ台
kamera dai
camera crane

カメラマン
kameraman
cameraman

関連用語 kanrenyōgo • vocabulary

チャンネル channeru **channel**	ニュース nyūsu **news**	新聞 shimbun **press**	連続ドラマ renzoku dorama **soap**	アニメ anime **cartoon**	ライブ raibu **live**
番組制作 bangumi seisaku **programming**	ドキュメンタリー dokyumentarī **documentary**	シリーズ番組 shirīzu bangumi **television series**	ゲーム番組 gēmu bangumi **game show**	録画 rokuga **prerecorded**	放送する hōsō suru **broadcast (v)**

インタビュアー intabyuā
interviewer

レポーター repōtā | reporter

テロップ teroppu |
teleprompter

ニュースキャスター
nyūsukyasutā | news anchor

俳優 haiyū | actors

ブームマイク būmumaiku
sound boom

カチンコ kachinko
clapper board

映画のセット eiga no setto
film set

ラジオ rajio • radio

調整卓
chōsei taku
mixing desk

マイク
maiku
microphone

サウンドエンジニア
saundo enjinia
sound technician

録音スタジオ rokuon sutajio | recording studio

関連用語 kanrenyōgo • vocabulary

ラジオ局
rajio kyoku
radio station

中波
chūha
medium wave

放送
hōsō
broadcast

周波数
shūhasū
frequency

波長
hachō
wavelength

音量
onryō
volume

長波
chōha
long wave

合わせる
awaseru
tune (v)

短波
tampa
short wave

ディスクジョッキー
disuku jokkī
DJ

法律 hōritsu • law

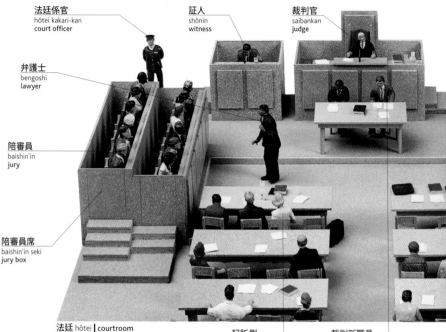

法廷係官
hōtei kakari-kan
court officer

証人
shōnin
witness

裁判官
saibankan
judge

弁護士
bengoshi
lawyer

陪審員
baishin'in
jury

陪審員席
baishin'in seki
jury box

法廷 hōtei | courtroom

起訴側
kiso-gawa
prosecution

裁判所職員
saibansho shokuin
court official

関連用語 kanrenyōgo • vocabulary

法律事務所 hōritsu jimusho **lawyer's office**	呼出し状 yobidashijō **summons**	命令 meirei **writ**	訴訟案件 soshō anken **court case**
法律相談 hōritsu sōdan **legal advice**	陳述書 chinjutsu-sho **statement**	公判日 kōhan-bi **court date**	罪状 zaijō **charge**
クライアント kuraianto **client**	令状 reijō **warrant**	罪状認否 zaijōnimpi **plea**	被疑者 higisha **accused**

速記者
sokki-sha
stenographer

容疑者
yōgisha
suspect

犯罪者
hanzai-sha
criminal

被告人
hikokunin
defendant

被告側
hikoku-gawa
defense

モンタージュ写真 montāju
shashin | **composite**

犯罪歴 hanzai-reki
criminal record

看守 kanshu | **prison guard**

監房 kambō | **cell**

刑務所 keimusho | **prison**

関連用語 kanrenyōgo • vocabulary

証拠 shōko **evidence**	有罪 yūzai **guilty**	保釈金 hoshakukin **bail**	弁護士に会わせてください。 bengoshi ni awasete kudasai **I want to see a lawyer.**
判決 hanketsu **verdict**	無罪 muzai **acquitted**	上訴 jōso **appeal**	裁判所はどこですか。 saibansho wa doko desuka? **Where is the courthouse?**
無実 mujitsu **innocent**	刑罰 keibatsu **sentence**	仮釈放 karishakuhō **parole**	保釈金を払えますか。 hoshakukin o haraemasuka? **Can I post bail?**

農場1 nōjō • farm 1

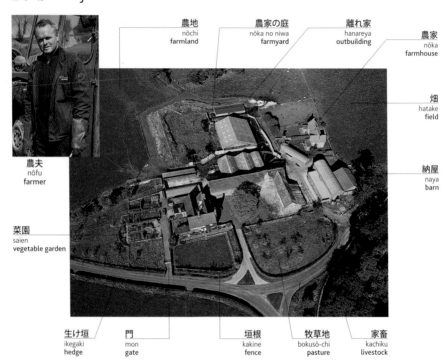

農夫
nōfu
farmer

農地
nōchi
farmland

農家の庭
nōka no niwa
farmyard

離れ家
hanareya
outbuilding

農家
nōka
farmhouse

畑
hatake
field

納屋
naya
barn

菜園
saien
vegetable garden

生け垣
ikegaki
hedge

門
mon
gate

垣根
kakine
fence

牧草地
bokusō-chi
pasture

家畜
kachiku
livestock

耕運機
kō'unki
cultivator

トラクター torakutā | tractor

コンバイン kombain | combine

農場の種類 nōjō no shurui ● types of farm

作物
sakumotsu
crop

羊の群れ
hitsuji no mure
flock

耕作農場
kōsaku nōjō
crop farm

酪農場
rakunōjō
dairy farm

牧羊農場
bokuyō nōjō
sheep farm

養鶏場 yōkeijō
poultry farm

葡萄の木
budō no ki
vine

養豚場
yōtonjō
pig farm

養魚場
yōgyojō
fish farm

果樹園
kajuen
fruit farm

葡萄園
budōen
vineyard

業務 gyōmu ● actions

畦
aze
furrow

耕す
tagayasu
plow (v)

種を蒔く
tane o maku
sow (v)

乳を搾る
chichi o shiboru
milk (v)

餌を与える
esa o ataeru
feed (v)

水を引く mizu o hiku
water (v)

刈り入れる kari'ireru
harvest (v)

関連用語 kanrenyōgo ● vocabulary

除草剤
josōzai
herbicide

群れ
mure
herd

かいば桶
kaibaoke
trough

殺虫剤
satchūzai
pesticide

サイロ
sairo
silo

植える
ueru
plant (v)

農場2 nōjō • farm 2

作物 sakumotsu • crops

小麦
komugi
wheat

トウモロコシ
tōmorokoshi
corn

大麦
ōmugi
barley

菜種
natane
rapeseed

向日葵
himawari
sunflower

俵
tawara
bale

干し草
hoshikusa
hay

アルファルファ
arufarufa
alfalfa

煙草
tabako
tobacco

米
kome
rice

茶
cha
tea

コーヒー
kōhī
coffee

亜麻
ama
flax

砂糖黍
satōkibi
sugarcane

綿花
menka
cotton

かかし
kakashi
scarecrow

家畜 kachiku • livestock

子豚
kobuta
piglet

子牛
ko-ushi
calf

豚
buta
pig

雌牛
meushi
cow

雄牛
o-ushi
bull

羊
hitsuji
sheep

子山羊
koyagi
kid

子馬
ko-uma
foal

子羊
kohitsuji
lamb

山羊
yagi
goat

馬
uma
horse

驢馬
roba
donkey

雛
hiyoko
chick

子鴨
kogamo
duckling

鶏
niwatori
chicken

雄鶏
ondori
cockerel

七面鳥
shichimenchō
turkey

鴨
kamo
duck

馬屋
umaya
stable

畜舎
chikusha
pen

鳥小屋
torigoya
chicken coop

豚小屋
butagoya
pigsty

建設 kensetsu • construction

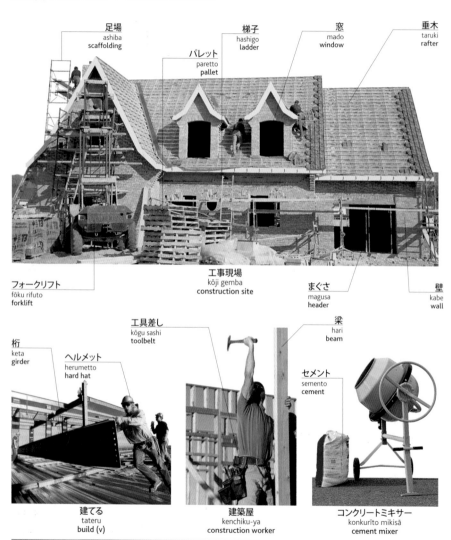

足場
ashiba
scaffolding

梯子
hashigo
ladder

窓
mado
window

垂木
taruki
rafter

パレット
paretto
pallet

工事現場
kōji gemba
construction site

フォークリフト
fōku rifuto
forklift

まぐさ
magusa
header

壁
kabe
wall

工具差し
kōgu sashi
toolbelt

梁
hari
beam

桁
keta
girder

ヘルメット
herumetto
hard hat

セメント
semento
cement

建てる
tateru
build (v)

建築屋
kenchiku-ya
construction worker

コンクリートミキサー
konkurīto mikisā
cement mixer

建築材料 kenchiku zairyō • materials

煉瓦
renga
brick

材木
zaimoku
lumber

屋根瓦
yane-gawara
roof tile

コンクリートブロック
konkurīto burokku
concrete block

道具 dōgu • tools

モルタル
morutaru
mortar

こて
kote
trowel

水平器
suiheiki
level

柄
e
handle

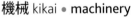
大ハンマー
ōhanmā
sledgehammer

つるはし
tsuruhashi
pickax

スコップ
sukoppu
shovel

機械 kikai • machinery

ローラー
rōrā
roller

ダンプカー
dampukā
dump truck

アウトリガー
autorigā
support

フック
fukku
hook

クレーン車 kurēn-sha I **crane**

道路工事 dōro kōji • roadwork

タールマック
tārumakku
asphalt

三角コーン
sankaku-kōn
cone

空気ドリル
kūki-doriru
pneumatic drill

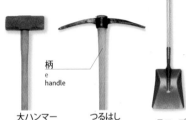

再舗装
saihosō
resurfacing

掘削機
kussakuki
excavator

職業1 shokugyō • occupations 1

大工
daiku
carpenter

電気工
denkikō
electrician

配管工
haikankō
plumber

建築屋
kenchiku-ya
construction worker

庭師
niwashi
gardener

掃除機
sōjiki
vacuum
cleaner

掃除夫
sōjifu
cleaner

修理工
shūrikō
mechanic

肉屋
nikuya
butcher

鋏
hasami
scissors

魚屋
sakanaya
fishmonger

八百屋
yaoya
greengrocer

花屋
hanaya
florist

美容師
biyōshi
hair stylist

床屋
tokoya
barber

宝石商
hōseki-shō
jeweler

店員
ten'in
shop clerk

不動産屋
fudōsan-ya
real estate agent

眼鏡屋
megane-ya
optician

マスク
masuku
mask

歯医者
haisha
dentist

医者
isha
doctor

薬剤師
yakuzaishi
pharmacist

看護婦
kangofu
nurse

獣医
jūi
veterinarian

農夫
nōfu
farmer

漁師
ryōshi
fisherman

マシンガン
mashin-gan
machine gun

名札
nafuda
identity badge

制服
seifuku
uniform

警備員
keibi'in
security guard

船員
sen'in
sailor

兵士
heishi
soldier

警官
keikan
policeman

消防士
shōbōshi
firefighter

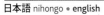

職業2 shokugyō • occupations 2

弁護士
bengoshi
lawyer

会計士
kaikeishi
accountant

模型
mokei
model

建築家 kenchikuka I architect

科学者
kagakusha
scientist

教師
kyōshi
teacher

司書
shisho
librarian

受付係
uketsuke gakari
receptionist

郵便鞄
yūbin kaban
mailbag

郵便配達
yūbinhaitatsu
mail carrier

バスの運転手
basu no untenshu
bus driver

トラックの運転手
torakku no untenshu
truck driver

タクシーの運転手
takushī no untenshu
taxi driver

パイロット
pairotto
pilot

スチュワーデス
suchuwādesu
air stewardess

旅行代理店の社員
ryokō dairiten no shain
travel agent

シェフの帽子
shefu no bōshi
chef's hat

シェフ
shefu
chef

チュチュ
chuchu
tutu

音楽家
ongakuka
musician

ダンサー
dansā
dancer

俳優
haiyū
actor

歌手
kashu
singer

ウェイトレス
weitoresu
waitress

バーテン
bāten
bartender

スポーツマン
supōtsuman
athlete

彫刻家
chōkokuka
sculptor

画家
gaka
painter

写真家
shashinka
photographer

ニュースキャスター
nyūsukyasutā
news anchor

メモ
memo
notes

ジャーナリスト
jānarisuto
journalist

編集者
henshū-sha
editor

デザイナー
dezainā
designer

針子
hariko
seamstress

仕立屋
shitateya
tailor

交通 kōtsū
transportation

道路 dōro • roads

高速道路
kōsoku dōro
highway

料金所
ryōkin-jo
toll booth

路面標識
romen hyōshiki
road markings

出入路
shutsunyū-ro
on-ramp

一方通行
ippōt-sūkō
one-way

分岐帯
bunki-tai
divider

ジャンクション
jankushon
junction

信号
shingō
traffic light

走行車線
sōkō shasen
inside lane

中央車線
chūō shasen
middle lane

追い越し車線
oikoshi shasen
outside lane

出口ランプ
deguchi rampu
exit ramp

交通
kōtsū
traffic

高架道路
kōka dōro
overpass

路肩
rokata
hard shoulder

トラック
torakku
truck

中央分離帯
chūō bunri-tai
median

ガード下通路
gādo shita tsūro
underpass

緊急電話
kinkyū denwa
emergency phone

身体障害者用駐車スペース
shintaishōgaisha-yō
chūsha supēsu
disabled parking

横断歩道
ōdan hodō
pedestrian crossing

交通渋滞
kōtsū jūtai
traffic jam

地図
chizu
map

パーキングメーター
pākingu mētā
parking meter

交通巡査
kōtsū junsa
traffic police officer

関連用語 kanrenyōgo • vocabulary

環状交差点 kanjō kōsaten traffic circle	往復分離道路 ōfuku bunri dōro divided highway	追い越す oikosu pass (v)
迂回路 ukairo diversion	駐車する chūsha suru park (v)	レッカー移動 rekkā idō tow away (v)
道路工事 dōro kōji roadwork	運転する unten suru drive (v)	これは...へ行く道ですか。 kore wa ... e iku michi desuka? Is this the road to...?
ガードレール gādo rēru crash barrier	バックする bakku suru back up (v)	どこに駐車できますか。 dokoni chūsha dekimasuka? Where can I park?

道路標識 dōro hyōshiki • road signs

進入禁止
shinnyū kinshi
do not enter

制限速度
seigen sokudo
speed limit

危険
kiken
hazard

停車禁止
teisha kinshi
no stopping

右折禁止
jusetsu kinshi
no right turn

バス basu • bus

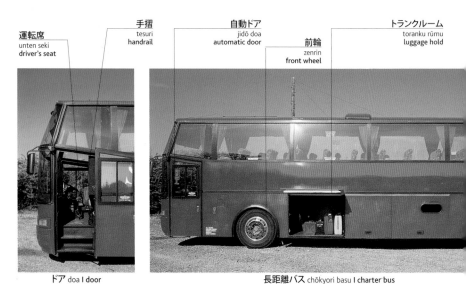

運転席
unten seki
driver's seat

手摺
tesuri
handrail

自動ドア
jidō doa
automatic door

前輪
zenrin
front wheel

トランクルーム
toranku rūmu
luggage hold

ドア doa I door

長距離バス chōkyori basu I charter bus

バスの種類 basu no shurui • types of buses

路線番号
rosen bangō
route number

運転手
untenshu
driver

二階建てバス
nikaidate basu
double-decker bus

路面電車
romen densha
tram

トロリーバス
tororī basu
trolley bus

スクールバス sukūru basu I school bus

後輪
kōrin
rear wheel

窓
mado
window

停車ボタン
teisha botan
stop button

乗車券
jōshaken
bus ticket

ベル
beru
bell

バスターミナル
basu tāminaru
bus station

バス停
basu-tei
bus stop

関連用語 kanrenyōgo • vocabulary

料金
ryōkin
fare

車椅子対応
kurumaisu taiō
wheelchair access

時刻表
jikokuhyō
timetable

バス待合所
basu machiai-jo
bus shelter

...で停まりますか。
... de tomarimasuka?
Do you stop at...?

...へ行くのは、どのバスですか。
... e ikunowa dono basu desuka?
Which bus goes to...?

マイクロバス
maikuro basu
minibus

観光バス kankō basu | tourist bus

シャトルバス shatoru basu | shuttle bus

自動車1 jidōsha • car 1

外装 gaisō • exterior

ドアミラー
doa mirā
side mirror

フロントガラス
furonto garasu
windshield

バックミラー
bakku mirā
rearview mirror

ワイパー
waipā
windshield wiper

ドア
doa
door

ボンネット
bonnetto
hood

トランク
toranku
trunk

方向指示器
hōkō shijiki
turn signal

バンパー
bampā
bumper

ヘッドライト
heddo raito
headlight

車輪
sharin
wheel

タイヤ
taiya
tire

ナンバープレート
nambā purēto
license plate

荷物
nimotsu
luggage

ルーフラック
rūfu rakku
roofrack

後部ドア
kōbu doa
tailgate

シートベルト
shīto beruto
seat belt

チャイルドシート
chairudo shīto
child seat

車の種類 kuruma no shurui • types

コンパクトカー
kompakuto kā
compact

ハッチバック
hatchibakku
hatchback

セダン
sedan
sedan

ステーションワゴン
sutēshonwagon
station wagon

オープンカー
ōpun kā
convertible

スポーツカー
supōtsu kā
sports car

ワンボックスカー
wambokkusu kā
minivan

四輪駆動車
yonrin kudōsha
four-wheel drive

クラシックカー
kurashikku kā
vintage

リムジン
rimujin
limousine

ガソリンスタンド gasorin sutando • gas station

ガソリンポンプ
gasorin pompu
pump

価格
kakaku
price

給油場
kyūyujō
forecourt

給気装置
kyūki sōchi
air supply

関連用語 kanrenyōgo • vocabulary

オイル oiru **oil**	有鉛 yūen **leaded**	洗車 sensha **car wash**
ガソリン gasorin **gasoline**	ディーゼル dīzeru **diesel**	不凍剤 futōzai **antifreeze**
無鉛 muen **unleaded**	整備工場 seibi kōjō **garage**	フロントガラス洗浄液 furonto-garasu senjōeki **windshield wash**

満タンお願いします。
mantan onegaishimasu.
Fill the tank, please.

自動車 2 jidōsha · car 2

内装 naisō · interior

後部座席
kōbu zaseki
back seat

アームレスト
āmu resuto
armrest

ヘッドレスト
heddo resuto
headrest

ドアロック
doa rokku
door lock

ドアハンドル
doa handoru
handle

関連用語 kanrenyōgo · vocabulary

ツードア tsū doa **two-door**	フォードア fō doa **four-door**	オートマ ōtoma **automatic**	ブレーキ burēki **brake**	アクセル akuseru **accelerator**
スリードア surī doa **three-door**	マニュアル manyuaru **manual**	イグニッション igunisshon **ignition**	クラッチ kuratchi **clutch**	エアコン eakon **air conditioning**

...への行き方を教えてください。
... eno ikikata o oshiete kudasai?
Can you tell me the way to...?

駐車場はどこですか。
chūshajō wa doko desuka?
Where is the parking lot?

ここに駐車できますか。
kokoni chūsha dekimasuka?
Can I park here?

操作系 sōsakei • controls

ハンドル	クラクション	ダッシュボード	ハザードランプ	カーナビ
handoru	kurakushon	dasshubōdo	hazādo rampu	kānabi
steering wheel	**horn**	**dashboard**	**hazard lights**	**satellite navigation**

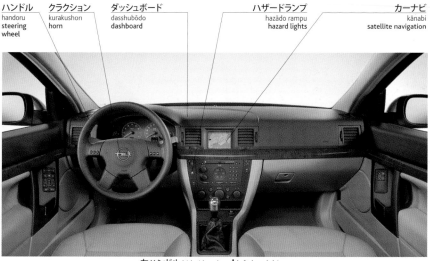

左ハンドル hidari handoru | left-hand drive

水温計
suionkei
temperature gauge

タコメーター
takomētā
tachometer

速度計
sokudokei
speedometer

燃料計
nenryōkei
fuel gauge

カーオーディオ
kā ōdio
car stereo

ライトスイッチ
raito suitchi
lights switch

オドメーター
odomētā
odometer

ヒーター調節
hītā chōsetsu
heater controls

エアバッグ
eabaggu
air bag

変速レバー
hensoku rebā
gearshift

右ハンドル migi handoru | right-hand drive

自動車 3 jidōsha • car 3

機械構造 kikaikōzō • mechanics

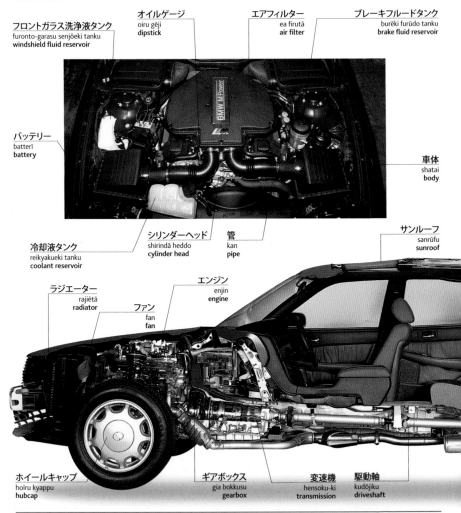

フロントガラス洗浄液タンク
furonto-garasu senjōeki tanku
windshield fluid reservoir

オイルゲージ
oiru gēji
dipstick

エアフィルター
ea firutā
air filter

ブレーキフルードタンク
burēki furūdo tanku
brake fluid reservoir

バッテリー
batterī
battery

車体
shatai
body

冷却液タンク
reikyakueki tanku
coolant reservoir

シリンダーヘッド
shirindā heddo
cylinder head

管
kan
pipe

サンルーフ
sanrūfu
sunroof

ラジエーター
rajiētā
radiator

エンジン
enjin
engine

ファン
fan
fan

ホイールキャップ
hoīru kyappu
hubcap

ギアボックス
gia bokkusu
gearbox

変速機
hensoku-ki
transmission

駆動軸
kudōjiku
driveshaft

パンク panku • puncture

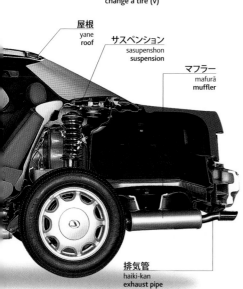

スペアタイヤ
supea taiya
spare tire

レンチ
renchi
tire iron

ホイールナット
hoīru natto
lug nuts

ジャッキ
jakki
jack

タイヤを交換する
taiya o kōkan suru
change a tire (v)

屋根
yane
roof

サスペンション
sasupenshon
suspension

マフラー
mafurā
muffler

排気管
haiki-kan
exhaust pipe

関連用語 kanrenyōgo • vocabulary

自動車事故
jidōsha jiko
car accident

燃料タンク
nenryō tanku
gas tank

故障
koshō
breakdown

タイミング
taimingu
timing

保険
hoken
insurance

ターボチャージャー
tābochājā
turbocharger

牽引車
ken'insha
tow truck

配電器
haidenki
distributor

修理工
shūrikō
mechanic

シャシー
shashī
chassis

タイヤ空気圧
taiya kūkiatsu
tire pressure

ハンドブレーキ
handoburēki
handbrake

ヒューズボックス
hyūzu bokkusu
fuse box

オルタネータ
orutanēta
alternator

スパークプラグ
supāku puragu
spark plug

カムベルト
kamu beruto
cam belt

ファンベルト
fam beruto
fan belt

. . . .

車が故障しました。
kuruma ga koshō shimashita.
I've broken down.

車がスタートしません。
kuruma ga sutāto shimasen.
My car won't start.

修理はできますか。
shūri wa dekimasuka?
Do you do repairs?

エンジンがオーバーヒートしています。
enjin ga ōbāhīto shite imasu.
The engine is overheating.

オートバイ ōtobai • motorcycle

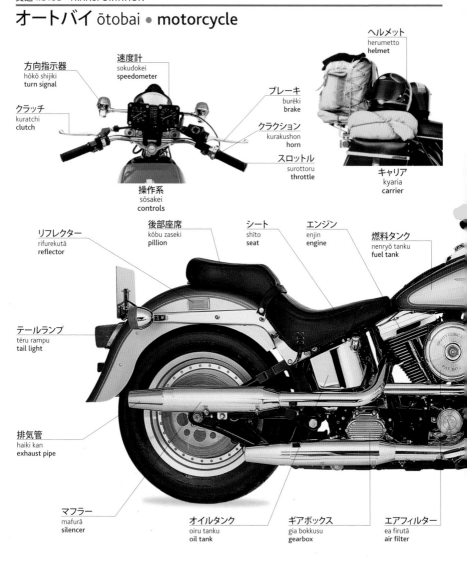

方向指示器
hōkō shijiki
turn signal

速度計
sokudokei
speedometer

ヘルメット
herumetto
helmet

クラッチ
kuratchi
clutch

ブレーキ
burēki
brake

クラクション
kurakushon
horn

スロットル
surottoru
throttle

操作系
sōsakei
controls

キャリア
kyaria
carrier

リフレクター
rifurekutā
reflector

後部座席
kōbu zaseki
pillion

シート
shīto
seat

エンジン
enjin
engine

燃料タンク
nenryō tanku
fuel tank

テールランプ
tēru rampu
tail light

排気管
haiki kan
exhaust pipe

マフラー
mafurā
silencer

オイルタンク
oiru tanku
oil tank

ギアボックス
gia bokkusu
gearbox

エアフィルター
ea firutā
air filter

バイザー
baizā
visor

革ジャン
kawajan
leathers

反射材
hanshazai
reflector strap

膝当て
hiza'ate
knee pad

バイクウエア baiku uea | clothing

ヘッドライト
heddo raito
headlight

サスペンション
sasupenshon
suspension

泥除け
doroyoke
mudguard

ブレーキペダル
burēki pedaru
brake pedal

アクスル
akusuru
axle

タイヤ
taiya
tire

種類 shurui • types

レーシングバイク rēshingu baiku | racing bike

ウインドシールド
uindo-shīrudo
windshield

ツアラー tsuarā | tourer

ダートバイク dāto baiku | dirt bike

スタンド
sutando
stand

スクーター sukūtā | scooter

自転車 jitensha • bicycle

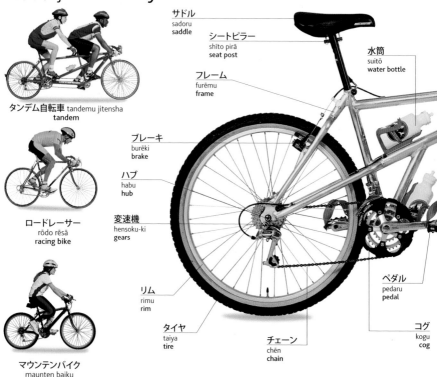

サドル
sadoru
saddle

シートピラー
shīto pirā
seat post

水筒
suitō
water bottle

フレーム
furēmu
frame

ブレーキ
burēki
brake

ハブ
habu
hub

変速機
hensoku-ki
gears

ペダル
pedaru
pedal

リム
rimu
rim

タイヤ
taiya
tire

チェーン
chēn
chain

コグ
kogu
cog

タンデム自転車 tandemu jitensha
tandem

ロードレーサー
rōdo rēsā
racing bike

マウンテンバイク
maunten baiku
mountain bike

ツーリング自転車
tsūringu jitensha
touring bike

ロードバイク
rōdo baiku
road bike

ヘルメット
herumetto
helmet

自転車道 jitensha-dō | **bicycle lane**

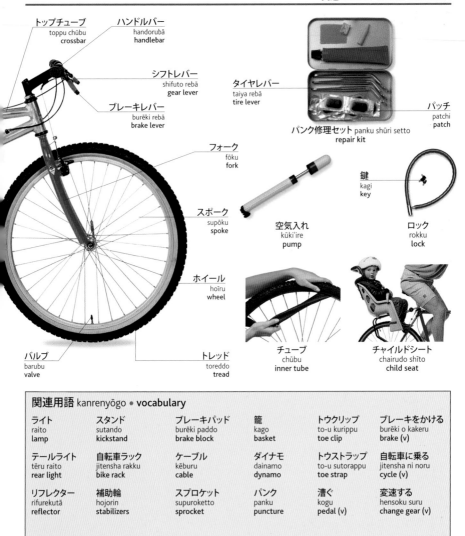

トップチューブ
toppu chūbu
crossbar

ハンドルバー
handorubā
handlebar

シフトレバー
shifuto rebā
gear lever

タイヤレバー
taiya rebā
tire lever

ブレーキレバー
burēki rebā
brake lever

パッチ
patchi
patch

パンク修理セット panku shūri setto
repair kit

フォーク
fōku
fork

鍵
kagi
key

スポーク
supōku
spoke

空気入れ
kūki'ire
pump

ロック
rokku
lock

ホイール
hoīru
wheel

チューブ
chūbu
inner tube

チャイルドシート
chairudo shīto
child seat

バルブ
barubu
valve

トレッド
toreddo
tread

関連用語 kanrenyōgo • vocabulary

ライト raito **lamp**	スタンド sutando **kickstand**	ブレーキパッド burēki paddo **brake block**	籠 kago **basket**	トウクリップ to-u kurippu **toe clip**	ブレーキをかける burēki o kakeru **brake (v)**
テールライト tēru raito **rear light**	自転車ラック jitensha rakku **bike rack**	ケーブル kēburu **cable**	ダイナモ dainamo **dynamo**	トウストラップ to-u sutorappu **toe strap**	自転車に乗る jitensha ni noru **cycle (v)**
リフレクター rifurekutā **reflector**	補助輪 hojorin **stabilizers**	スプロケット supuroketto **sprocket**	パンク panku **puncture**	漕ぐ kogu **pedal (v)**	変速する hensoku suru **change gear (v)**

列車 ressha • train

客車
kyakusha
car

ホーム
hōmu
platform

カート
kāto
cart

ホーム番号
hōmu bangō
platform number

通勤者
tsūkinsha
commuter

駅 eki | train station

列車の種類 ressha no shurui • types of train

エンジン
enjin
engine

蒸気機関車
jōki kikansha
steam train

運転室
unten shitsu
driver's cab

レール
rēru
rail

ディーゼル機関車 dīzeru kikansha | diesel train

電車
densha
electric train

高速列車
kōsoku ressha
high-speed train

モノレール
monorēru
monorail

地下鉄
chikatetsu
subway

路面電車
romen densha
tram

貨物列車
kamotsu ressha
freight train

網棚
amidana
luggage rack

車窓
shasō
window

線路
senro
track

改札口 kaisatsu-guchi | ticket gates

扉
tobira
door

座席
zaseki
seat

客室
kyakushitsu
compartment

拡声装置
kakusei sōchi
public address system

時刻表
jikokuhyō
timetable

切符
kippu
ticket

41213 KUPONG 7.00 kr

食堂車 shokudō-sha | dining car

コンコース konkōsu | concourse

寝台個室
shindai koshitsu
sleeping compartment

関連用語 kanrenyōgo • vocabulary

鉄道網 tetsudō-mō **rail network**	地下鉄路線図 chikatetsu rosenzu **subway map**	切符売場 kippu uriba **ticket office**	通電レール tsūden rēru **third rail**
インターシティ列車 intāshiti ressha **intercity train**	遅れ okure **delay**	検札員 kensatsuin **conductor**	信号 shingō **signal**
新幹線 shinkansen **bullet train**	料金 ryōkin **fare**	乗り換える norikaeru **change (v)**	非常レバー hijō rebā **emergency lever**

航空機 kōkūki ● aircraft

定期旅客機 teiki-ryokakki ● airliner

機首
kishu
nose

操縦室
sōjū shitsu
cockpit

エンジン
enjin
engine

機体
kitai
fuselage

翼
tsubasa
wing

尾翼
biyoku
tail

方向舵
hōkōda
rudder

ドア
doa
exit

前輪
zenrin
nosewheel

着陸装置
chakuriku sōchi
landing gear

補助翼
hojoyoku
aileron

垂直安定板
suichoku-anteiban
fin

水平尾翼
suihei-biyoku
tailplane

キャビン kyabin ● cabin

非常口
hijō guchi
emergency exit

乗務員
jōmuin
flight attendant

荷物入れ
nimotsuire
overhead locker

窓
mado
window

換気口
kankikō
air vent

座席
zaseki
seat

読書灯
dokusho-tō
reading light

列
retsu
row

肘掛け
hijikake
armrest

通路
tsūro
aisle

テーブル
tēburu
tray-table

背もたれ
semotare
seat back

マイクロライト
maikuroraito
ultralight

グライダー
guraidā
glider

複葉機
fukuyōki
biplane

プロペラ
puropera
propeller

熱気球
netsukikyū
hot-air balloon

軽飛行機
keihikōki
light aircraft

水上飛行機
suijō hikōki
sea plane

自家用ジェット機
jikayō jettoki
private jet

超音波ジェット機
chōompa jettoki
supersonic jet

ローターブレード
rōtā burēdo
rotor blade

ミサイル
misairu
missile

ヘリコプター
herikoputā
helicopter

爆撃機
bakugekiki
bomber

戦闘機
sentōki
fighter plane

関連用語 kanrenyōgo • vocabulary

パイロット pairotto **pilot**	離陸する ririku suru **takeoff (v)**	着陸する chakuriku suru **land (v)**	エコノミークラス ekonomī kurasu **economy class**	手荷物 tenimotsu **hand luggage**
副操縦士 fukusōjūshi **copilot**	飛ぶ tobu **fly (v)**	高度 kōdo **altitude**	ビジネスクラス bijinesu kurasu **business class**	シートベルト shīto beruto **seat belt**

空港 kūkō • airport

エプロン
epuron
apron

牽引車
ken'insha
baggage trailer

ターミナル
tāminaru
terminal

作業車
sagyō-sha
service vehicle

通路
tsūro
walkway

定期旅客機 teiki ryokakki | airliner

関連用語 kanrenyōgo • vocabulary

滑走路 kassōro **runway**	便名 binmei **flight number**	カルーセル karūseru **carousel**	休暇 kyūka **vacation**
国際便 kokusai bin **international flight**	出入国管理 shutsunyūkoku kanri **immigration**	警備 keibi **security**	チェックインする chekkuin suru **check in (v)**
国内便 kokunai bin **domestic flight**	税関 zeikan **customs**	レントゲン検査装置 rentogen kensa sōchi **x-ray machine**	管制塔 kanseitō **control tower**
乗り継ぎ noritsugi **connection**	超過荷物 chōka nimotsu **excess baggage**	旅行パンフレット ryokō panfuretto **travel brochure**	飛行機を予約する hikōki o yoyaku suru **book a flight (v)**

ビザ
biza
visa

旅券 ryoken | passport

手荷物
tenimotsu
hand luggage

荷物
nimotsu
luggage

カート
kāto
cart

チェックインデスク
chekuin desuku
check-in desk

入国審査
nyūkoku shinsa
passport control

搭乗券
tōjōken
boarding pass

航空券
kōkūken
ticket

ゲート番号
gēto bangō
gate number

出発便
shuppatsu bin
departures

出発ロビー
shuppatsu robī
departure lounge

目的地
mokutekichi
destination

到着便
tōchaku bin
arrivals

案内板
annai-ban
information screen

免税店
menzeiten
duty-free shop

荷物引き渡し
nimotsu hikiwatashi
baggage claim

タクシー乗り場
takushī noriba
cab stand

レンタカー
rentakā
car rental

船 fune • ship

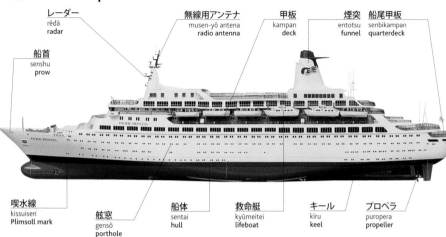

レーダー rēdā **radar**	無線用アンテナ musen-yō antena **radio antenna**	甲板 kampan **deck**
	煙突 entotsu **funnel**	船尾甲板 senbikampan **quarterdeck**

船首
senshu
prow

喫水線
kissuisen
Plimsoll mark

舷窓
gensō
porthole

船体
sentai
hull

救命艇
kyūmeitei
lifeboat

キール
kīru
keel

プロペラ
puropera
propeller

海洋定期船 kaiyō teikisen | ocean liner

船橋
senkyō
bridge

機関室
kikan shitsu
engine room

船室
senshitsu
cabin

調理室
chōri shitsu
galley

関連用語 kanrenyōgo • vocabulary

ドック
dokku
dock

港湾
kōwan
port

舷門
genmon
gangway

錨
ikari
anchor

係船柱
keisenchū
bollard

ウィンドラス
windorasu
windlass

船長
senchō
captain

高速モーターボート
kōsoku mōtābōto
speedboat

ボート
bōto
rowboat

カヌー
kanū
canoe

その他の船舶 sonota no sempaku • other ships

フェリー
ferī
ferry

船外機
sengaiki
outboard motor

ゴムボート
gomubōto
inflatable dinghy

水中翼船
suichūyoku-sen
hydrofoil

ヨット
yotto
yacht

カタマラン
katamaran
catamaran

曳航船
eikō-sen
tugboat

ホバークラフト
hobākurafuto
hovercraft

コンテナ船
kontena-sen
container ship

索具
sakugu
rigging

船倉
sensō
hold

帆船
hansen
sailboat

貨物船
kamotsu-sen
freighter

石油タンカー
sekiyu tankā
oil tanker

航空母艦
kōkū bokan
aircraft carrier

戦艦
senkan
battleship

展望塔
tembōtō
conning tower

潜水艦
sensuikan
submarine

港湾 kōwan · port

倉庫
sōko
warehouse

クレーン
kurēn
crane

フォークリフト
fōkurifuto
fork-lift

出入道路
shutsunyū dōro
access road

税関
zeikan
customs house

ドック
dokku
dock

コンテナ
kontena
container

波止場
hatoba
quay

貨物
kamotsu
cargo

フェリー乗り場
ferī noriba
ferry terminal

フェリー
ferī
ferry

切符売場
kippu uriba
ticket office

船客
senkyaku
passenger

コンテナ港 kontena-kō | container port

船客港 senkyaku-kō | passenger port

網
ami
net

漁船
gyosen
fishing boat

係留索具
keiryū sakugu
mooring

マリーナ marīna | marina

漁港 gyokō | fishing port

港 minato | harbor

桟橋 sambashi | pier

防波堤
bōhatei
jetty

造船所
zōsen jo
shipyard

ランプ
rampu
lamp

灯台
tōdai
lighthouse

ブイ
bui
buoy

関連用語 kanrenyōgo • vocabulary

沿岸警備隊
engan keibitai
coastguard

港長
kōchō
harbour master

錨を下ろす
ikari o orosu
drop anchor (v)

乾ドック
kandokku
dry dock

係留する
keiryū suru
moor (v)

波止場につける
hatoba ni tsukeru
dock (v)

乗船する
jōsen suru
board (v)

下船する
gesen suru
disembark (v)

出港する
shukkō suru
set sail (v)

スポーツ supōtsu
sports

アメリカンフットボール amerikan futtobōru
• American football

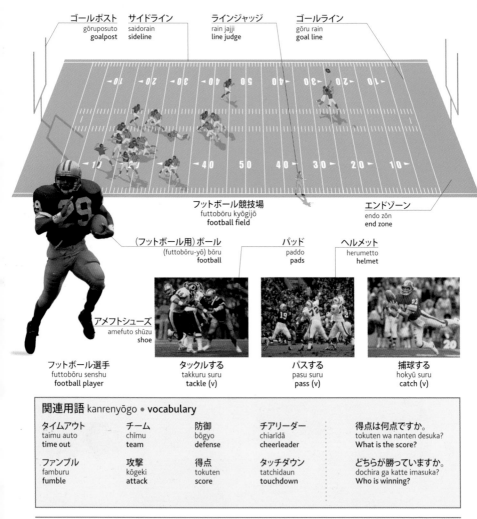

ゴールポスト
gōruposuto
goalpost

サイドライン
saidorain
sideline

ラインジャッジ
rain jajji
line judge

ゴールライン
gōru rain
goal line

フットボール競技場
futtobōru kyōgijō
football field

エンドゾーン
endo zōn
end zone

（フットボール用）ボール
(futtobōru-yō) bōru
football

パッド
paddo
pads

ヘルメット
herumetto
helmet

アメフトシューズ
amefuto shūzu
shoe

フットボール選手
futtobōru senshu
football player

タックルする
takkuru suru
tackle (v)

パスする
pasu suru
pass (v)

捕球する
hokyū suru
catch (v)

関連用語 kanrenyōgo • vocabulary

タイムアウト taimu auto **time out**	**チーム** chīmu **team**	**防御** bōgyo **defense**	**チアリーダー** chiarīdā **cheerleader**	**得点は何点ですか。** tokuten wa nanten desuka? **What is the score?**
ファンブル famburu **fumble**	**攻撃** kōgeki **attack**	**得点** tokuten **score**	**タッチダウン** tatchidaun **touchdown**	**どちらが勝っていますか。** dochira ga katte imasuka? **Who is winning?**

ラグビー ragubī • rugby

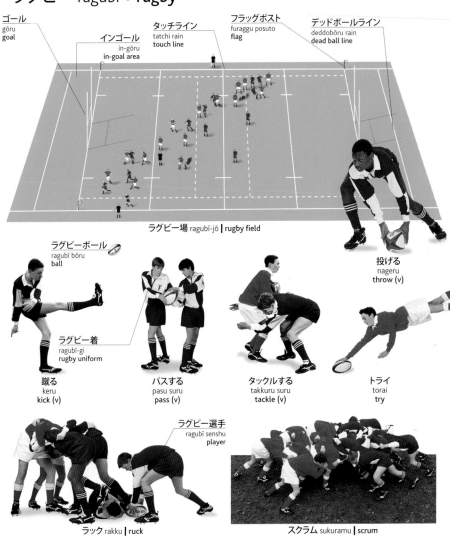

ゴール
gōru
goal

インゴール
in-gōru
in-goal area

タッチライン
tatchi rain
touch line

フラッグポスト
furaggu posuto
flag

デッドボールライン
deddobōru rain
dead ball line

ラグビー場 ragubī-jō | rugby field

ラグビーボール
ragubī bōru
ball

ラグビー着
ragubī-gi
rugby uniform

蹴る
keru
kick (v)

パスする
pasu suru
pass (v)

タックルする
takkuru suru
tackle (v)

トライ
torai
try

投げる
nageru
throw (v)

ラグビー選手
ragubī senshu
player

ラック rakku | ruck

スクラム sukuramu | scrum

サッカー sakkā • soccer

サッカーボール
sakkā bōru
soccer ball

ゴールキーパー
gōrukīpā
goalkeeper

フォワード
fowādo
forward

審判
shimpan
referee

センターサークル
sentā sākuru
center circle

サッカー 着
sakkā-gi
soccer uniform

サッカー選手
sakkā senshu
soccer player

サッカー場
sakkā-jō
soccer field

ゴールポスト
gōruposuto
goalpost

ネット
netto
net

クロスバー
kurosubā
crossbar

ドリブルする doriburu suru
dribble (v)

ヘディングする
hedingu suru
head (v)

壁
kabe
wall

ゴール gōru | goal

フリーキック furī kikku | free kick

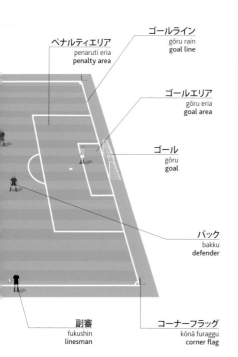

ペナルティエリア
penaruti eria
penalty area

ゴールライン
gōru rain
goal line

ゴールエリア
gōru eria
goal area

ゴール
gōru
goal

バック
bakku
defender

副審
fukushin
linesman

コーナーフラッグ
kōnā furaggu
corner flag

スローイン surō-in
throw-in

蹴る keru | **kick (v)**

サッカーシューズ
sakkā shūzu
boot

送球する
sōkyū suru
pass (v)

シュートする
shūto suru
shoot (v)

セーブする
sēbu suru
save (v)

タックルする
takkuru suru
tackle (v)

関連用語 kanrenyōgo • vocabulary

競技場 kyōgijō **stadium**	**ファウル** fauru **foul**	**イエローカード** ierō kādo **yellow card**	**連盟** renmei **league**	**延長時間** enchō jikan **extra time**
1点あげる itten ageru **score a goal (v)**	**コーナーキック** kōnā kikku **corner**	**オフサイド** ofu-saido **off-side**	**引分け** hikiwake **draw**	**補欠選手** hoketsusenshu **substitute**
ペナルティー penarutī **penalty**	**レッドカード** reddo kādo **red card**	**退場する** taijō suru **send off (v)**	**ハーフタイム** hāfu taimu **half time**	**代理** dairi **substitution**

ホッケー hokkē • hockey

アイスホッケー aisu hokkē • ice hockey

ディフェンディングゾーン
difendingu zōn
defending zone

ゴールライン
gōru rain
goal line

アタッキングゾーン
atakkingu zōn
attack zone

ニュートラルゾーン
nyūtoraru zōn
neutral zone

ゴールキーパー
gōrukīpā
goalkeeper

ゴール
gōru
goal

フェースオフサークル
fēsu-ofu sākuru
face-off circle

センターサークル
sentā sākuru
center circle

グローブ
gurōbu
glove

ショルダーパッド
shorudā paddo
pad

スケート
sukēto
ice skate

アイスホッケー用リンク
aisuhokkē-yō rinku
hockey rink

スティック
sutikku
stick

フィールドホッケー fīrudo hokkē • field hockey

ホッケー用スティック
hokkē-yō sutikku
hockey stick

パック
pakku
puck

アイスホッケー選手 aisuhokkē senshu
ice hockey player

ボール
bōru
ball

スケートで滑る
sukēto de suberu
skate (v)

打つ
utsu
hit (v)

クリケット kuriketto • cricket

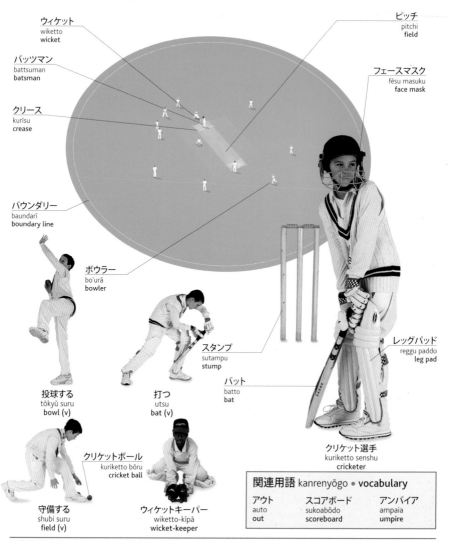

ウィケット
wiketto
wicket

バッツマン
battsuman
batsman

クリース
kurīsu
crease

バウンダリー
baundarī
boundary line

ボウラー
bo'urā
bowler

投球する
tōkyū suru
bowl (v)

守備する
shubi suru
field (v)

クリケットボール
kuriketto bōru
cricket ball

打つ
utsu
bat (v)

スタンプ
sutampu
stump

ウィケットキーパー
wiketto-kīpā
wicket-keeper

バット
batto
bat

ピッチ
pitchi
field

フェースマスク
fēsu masuku
face mask

レッグパッド
reggu paddo
leg pad

クリケット選手
kuriketto senshu
cricketer

関連用語 kanrenyōgo • vocabulary		
アウト	スコアボード	アンパイア
auto	sukoabōdo	ampaia
out	**scoreboard**	**umpire**

バスケットボール basukettobōru • basketball

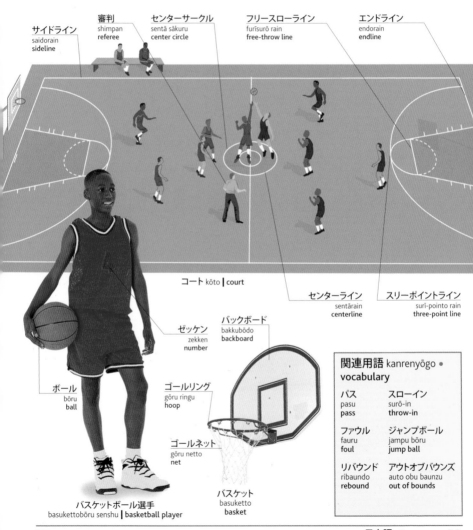

サイドライン
saidorain
sideline

審判
shimpan
referee

センターサークル
sentā sākuru
center circle

フリースローライン
furīsurō rain
free-throw line

エンドライン
endorain
endline

コート kōto | court

センターライン
sentārain
centerline

スリーポイントライン
surī-pointo rain
three-point line

ゼッケン
zekken
number

バックボード
bakkubōdo
backboard

ボール
bōru
ball

ゴールリング
gōru ringu
hoop

ゴールネット
gōru netto
net

バスケット
basuketto
basket

バスケットボール選手
basukettobōru senshu | basketball player

関連用語 kanrenyōgo • vocabulary

パス pasu pass	**スローイン** surō-in throw-in
ファウル fauru foul	**ジャンプボール** jampu bōru jump ball
リバウンド ribaundo rebound	**アウトオブバウンズ** auto obu baunzu out of bounds

動作 dōsa • actions

投げる
nageru
throw (v)

受ける
ukeru
catch (v)

シュートする
shūto suru
shoot (v)

ジャンプする
jampu suru
jump (v)

マークする
māku suru
mark (v)

ブロックする
burokku suru
block (v)

バウンドする
baundo suru
bounce (v)

ダンクシュートする
dankushūto suru
dunk (v)

バレーボール barēbōru • volleyball

ブロックする
burokku suru
block (v)

ネット
netto
net

レシーブする
reshību suru
dig (v)

審判
shimpan
referee

サポーター
sapōtā
knee support

コート kōto | court

野球 yakyū ● baseball

球場 kyūjō ● field

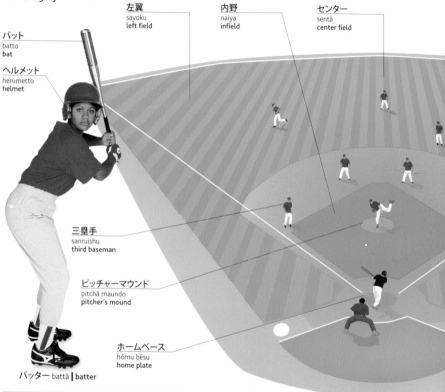

左翼
sayoku
left field

内野
naiya
infield

センター
sentā
center field

バット
batto
bat

ヘルメット
herumetto
helmet

三塁手
sanruishu
third baseman

ピッチャーマウンド
pitchā maundo
pitcher's mound

ホームベース
hōmu bēsu
home plate

バッター battā | batter

関連用語 kanrenyōgo ● vocabulary

イニング iningu inning	セーフ sēfu safe	ファウルボール fauru bōru foul ball
ラン ran run	アウト auto out	ストライク sutoraiku strike

ボール
bōru
ball

ミット mitto
mitt

マスク masuku
mask

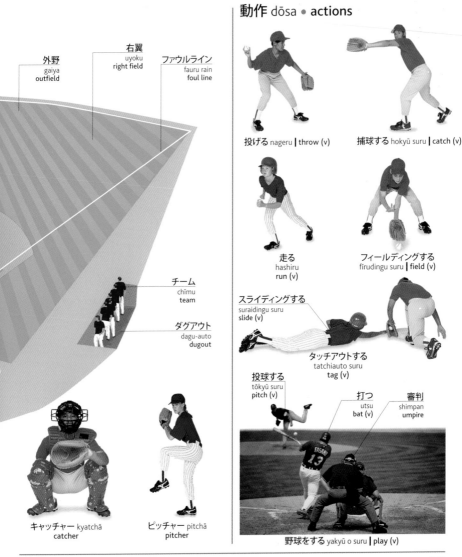

外野
gaiya
outfield

右翼
uyoku
right field

ファウルライン
fauru rain
foul line

動作 dōsa • actions

投げる nageru | throw (v)

捕球する hokyū suru | catch (v)

走る
hashiru
run (v)

フィールディングする
fīrudingu suru | field (v)

スライディングする
suraidingu suru
slide (v)

タッチアウトする
tatchiauto suru
tag (v)

投球する
tōkyū suru
pitch (v)

打つ
utsu
bat (v)

審判
shimpan
umpire

チーム
chīmu
team

ダグアウト
dagu-auto
dugout

キャッチャー kyatchā
catcher

ピッチャー pitchā
pitcher

野球をする yakyū o suru | play (v)

テニス tenisu • tennis

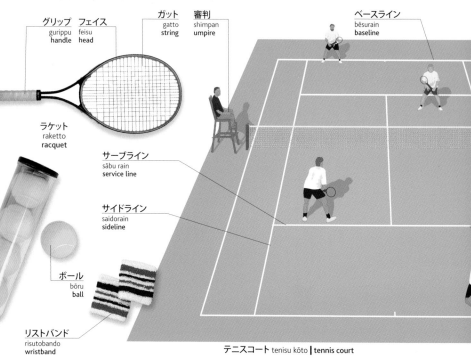

グリップ
gurippu
handle

フェイス
feisu
head

ガット
gatto
string

審判
shimpan
umpire

ベースライン
bēsurain
baseline

ラケット
raketto
racquet

サーブライン
sābu rain
service line

サイドライン
saidorain
sideline

ボール
bōru
ball

リストバンド
risutobando
wristband

テニスコート tenisu kōto | **tennis court**

関連用語 kanrenyōgo • vocabulary

シングルス shingurusu **singles**	セット setto **set**	ラブ rabu **love**	フォルト foruto **fault**	スライス suraisu **slice**	線審 senshin **linesman**
ダブルス daburusu **doubles**	マッチ matchi **match**	デュース dyūsu **deuce**	エース ēsu **ace**	ラリー rarī **rally**	選手権 senshuken **championship**
ゲーム gēmu **game**	タイブレーク taiburēku **tiebreak**	アドバンテージ adobantēji **advantage**	ドロップショット doroppu shotto **dropshot**	レット retto! **let!**	スピン supin **spin**

ストローク sutorōku • strokes

ネット
netto
net

スマッシュ
sumasshu
smash

ボールボーイ
bōrubŏi
ballboy

サーブ する
sābu suru
serve (v)

サーブ
sābu
serve

ボレー
borĕ
volley

リターン
ritān
return

ロブ
robu
lob

フォアハンド
foahando
forehand

バックハンド
bakkuhando
backhand

テニス靴
tenisu-gutsu
tennis shoes

テニス選手 tenisu senshu | **player**

ラケットスポーツ raketto supōtsu • racquet games

シャトル
shatoru
shuttlecock

ラケット
raketto
bat

バドミントン
badominton
badminton

卓球
takkyū
table tennis

スカッシュ
sukasshu
squash

ラケットボール
rakettobōru
racquetball

ゴルフ gorufu ● golf

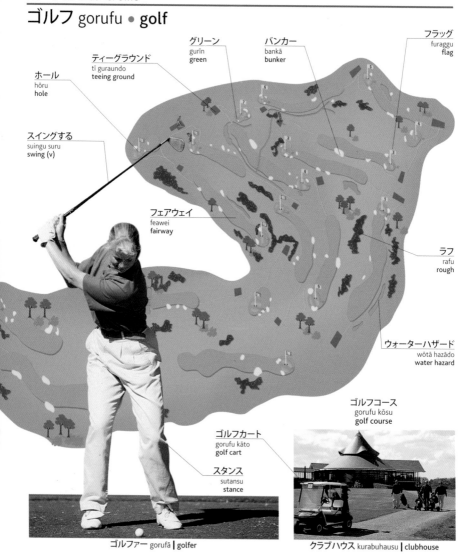

ホール
hōru
hole

スイングする
suingu suru
swing (v)

ティーグラウンド
tī guraundo
teeing ground

グリーン
gurīn
green

バンカー
bankā
bunker

フラッグ
furaggu
flag

フェアウェイ
feawei
fairway

ラフ
rafu
rough

ウォーターハザード
wōtā hazādo
water hazard

ゴルフコース
gorufu kōsu
golf course

ゴルフカート
gorufu kāto
golf cart

スタンス
sutansu
stance

ゴルファー gorufā | golfer

クラブハウス kurabuhausu | clubhouse

用具 yōgu • equipment

ゴルフボール
gorufu bōru
golf ball

傘
kasa
umbrella

ティー
tī
tee

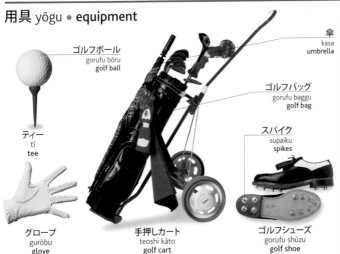

ゴルフバッグ
gorufu baggu
golf bag

スパイク
supaiku
spikes

グローブ
gurōbu
glove

手押しカート
teoshi kāto
golf cart

ゴルフシューズ
gorufu shūzu
golf shoe

ゴルフクラブ
gorufu kurabu
• golf clubs

ウッド
uddo
wood

パター
patā
putter

アイアン
aian
iron

ウェッジ
wejji
wedge

動作 dōsa • actions

ティーショットを打ち出す
tīshotto o uchidasu
tee-off (v)

ドライバーショットを打つ
doraibāshotto o utsu
drive (v)

パットを打つ
patto o utsu
putt (v)

チップショットを打つ
chippushotto o utsu
chip (v)

関連用語 kanrenyōgo • vocabulary

ホールインワン hōru in wan **hole in one**	パー pā **par**	ハンディキャップ handikyappu **handicap**	キャディ kyadi **caddy**	バックスイング bakkusuingu **backswing**	ストローク sutorōku **stroke**
アンダーパー andā pā **under par**	オーバーパー ōbā pā **over par**	トーナメント tōnamento **tournament**	観衆 kanshū **spectators**	素振り suburi **practice swing**	プレーの線 purē no sen **line of play**

陸上競技 rikujō kyōgi • track and field

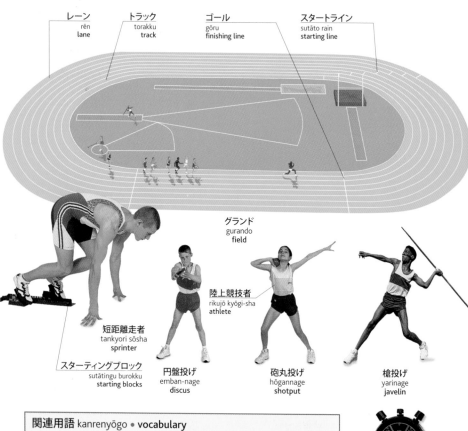

レーン rēn **lane**	トラック torakku **track**	ゴール gōru **finishing line**	スタートライン sutāto rain **starting line**

グランド
gurando
field

陸上競技者
rikujō kyōgi-sha
athlete

短距離走者
tankyori sōsha
sprinter

スターティングブロック
sutātingu burokku
starting blocks

円盤投げ
emban-nage
discus

砲丸投げ
hōgannage
shotput

槍投げ
yarinage
javelin

関連用語 kanrenyōgo • vocabulary

競争 kyōsō **race**	記録 kiroku **record**	写真判定 shashin hantei **photo finish**	棒高跳び bōtakatobi **pole vault**
時間 jikan **time**	記録を破る kiroku o yaburu **break a record (v)**	マラソン marason **marathon**	自己最高記録 jiko saikō kiroku **personal best**

ストップウォッチ
sutoppuwotchi
stopwatch

バトン
baton
baton

リレー競争
rirē kyōsō
relay race

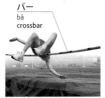

バー
bā
crossbar

走り高跳び
hashiritakatobi
high jump

走り幅跳び
hashirihabatobi
long jump

ハードル走
hādorusō
hurdles

体操競技 taisō kyōgi • gymnastics

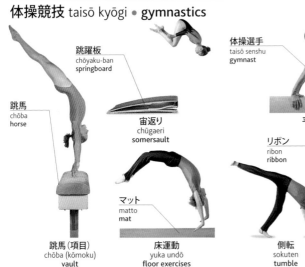

跳躍板
chōyaku-ban
springboard

跳馬
chōba
horse

宙返り
chūgaeri
somersault

マット
matto
mat

体操選手
taisō senshu
gymnast

平均台 heikindai | **beam**

リボン
ribon
ribbon

跳馬（項目）
chōba (kōmoku)
vault

床運動
yuka undō
floor exercises

側転
sokuten
tumble

新体操
shintaisō
rhythmic gymnastics

関連用語 kanrenyōgo • vocabulary

鉄棒 tetsubō horizontal bar	**鞍馬** amba pommel horse	**吊り輪** tsuriwa rings	**メダル** medaru medals	**銀** gin silver
平行棒 heikōbō parallel bars	**段違い平行棒** danchigai heikōbō asymmetric bars	**表彰台** hyōshō dai podium	**金** kin gold	**銅** dō bronze

格闘技 kakutōgi • combat sports

相手
aite
opponent

ミット
mitto
glove

ヘッドガード
heddogādo
guard

帯
obi
belt

空手 karate | karate

テコンドー tekondō | tae-kwon-do

面
men
mask

柔道 jūdō | judo

竹刀
shinai
sword

合気道 aikidō | aikido

剣道 kendō | kendo

カンフー kanfū
kung fu

キックボクシング
kikkubokushingu | kickboxing

レスリング resuringu | wrestling

ボクシング bokushingu | boxing

技 waza • actions

袈裟固 kesagatame | fall

襟掴み erizukami | hold

投げ nage | throw

抑え osae | pin

蹴り keri | kick

突き tsuki | punch

払い harai | strike

手刀打ち shutō uchi | chop

飛び蹴り tobi-geri | jump

受け uke | block

関連用語 kanrenyōgo • vocabulary

リング ringu **boxing ring**	ラウンド raundo **round**	拳 kobushi **fist**	黒帯 kuro obi **black belt**	カポエイラ kapoeira **capoeira**
グローブ gurōbu **boxing gloves**	試合 shiai **bout**	ノックアウト nokku auto **knock out**	護身 goshin **self defense**	相撲 sumō **sumo wrestling**
マウスピース mausu pīsu **mouth guard**	練習試合 renshū-jiai **sparring**	パンチバッグ panchi baggu **punch bag**	武道 budō **martial arts**	太極拳 taikyokuken **tai-chi**

水泳 suiei ・ swimming
水泳用品 suiei yōhin ・ equipment

アームバンド
āmubando
armband

ゴーグル gōguru | goggles

鼻栓
hana sen
nose clip

スイムボード
suimubōdo | float

水着 mizugi | swimsuit

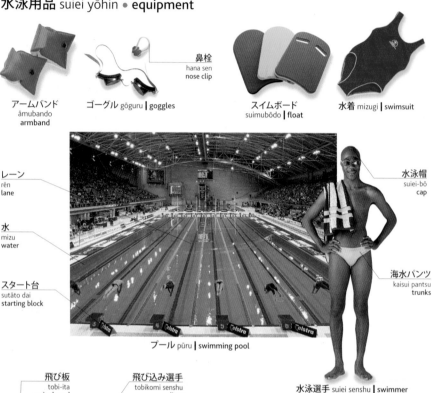

レーン
rēn
lane

水
mizu
water

スタート台
sutāto dai
starting block

水泳帽
suiei-bō
cap

海水パンツ
kaisui pantsu
trunks

プール pūru | swimming pool

飛び板
tobi-ita
springboard

飛び込み選手
tobikomi senshu
diver

水泳選手 suiei senshu | swimmer

飛び込む tobikomu | dive (v)

泳ぐ oyogu | swim (v)

回転 kaiten | turn

泳法 eihō • styles

クロール kurōru | front crawl

平泳ぎ hiraoyogi | breaststroke

かき
kaki
stroke

蹴り
keri
kick

背泳ぎ seoyogi | backstroke

バタフライ batafurai | butterfly

スキューバダイビング sukyūba daibingu • scuba diving

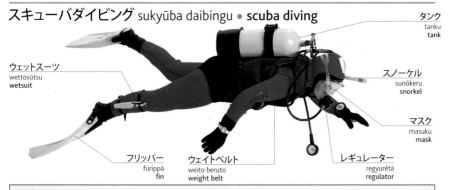

タンク
tanku
tank

ウェットスーツ
wettosūtsu
wetsuit

スノーケル
sunōkeru
snorkel

マスク
masuku
mask

フリッパー
furippā
fin

ウェイトベルト
weito beruto
weight belt

レギュレーター
regyurētā
regulator

関連用語 kanrenyōgo • vocabulary

飛び込み tobikomi dive	立ち泳ぎする tachioyogi suru tread water (v)	ロッカー rokkā lockers	水球 suikyū water polo	浅瀬 asase shallow end	こむら返り komuragaeri cramp
高飛び込み takatobikomi high dive	飛び込みスタート tobikomi sutāto racing dive	救助員 kyūjo-in lifeguard	深み fukami deep end	シンクロナイズドスイミング shinkuronaizudo suimingu synchronized swimming	溺れる oboreru drown (v)

セーリング sēringu ● sailing

コンパス
kompasu
compass

錨
ikari
anchor

ヘッドセール
heddosēru
headsail

クリート
kurīto
cleat

サイドデッキ
saido dekki
sidedeck

船首
senshu
bow

舵棒
kaji bō
tiller

船体
sentai
hull

マスト
masuto
mast

リギン
rigin
rigging

主帆
shuhan
mainsail

ブーム
būmu
boom

船尾
sembi
stern

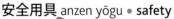

航行する kōkō suru | navigate (v)

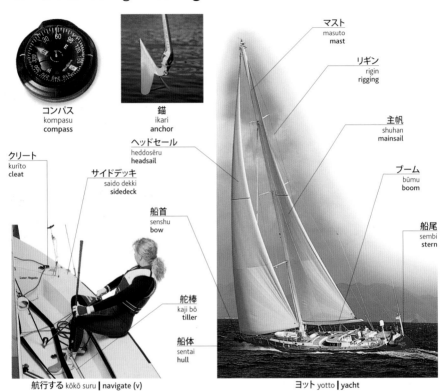

ヨット yotto | yacht

安全用具 anzen yōgu ● safety

照明弾
shōmeidan
flare

救命ブイ
kyūmei bui
lifebuoy

救命胴衣
kyūmei dōi
life jacket

救命ボート
kyūmei bōto
life raft

水上スポーツ suijō supōtsu • **watersports**

漕ぎ手
kogite
rower

オール
ōru
oar

カヤック
kayakku
kayak

パドル
padoru
paddle

漕ぐ kogu | row (v)

カヌー
kanū
canoeing

セール
sēru
sail

サーフボード
sāfubōdo
surfboard

水上スキー板
suijōsukī ita
ski

ウインドサーファー
uindosāfā
windsurfer

サーフィン
sāfin
surfing

水上スキー
suijōsukī
waterskiing

高速ボート
kōsoku bōto
speed boating

ボード
bōdo
board

フットストラップ
futtosutorappu
footstrap

ラフティング
rafutingu
rafting

ジェットスキー
jettosukī
jet skiing

ウインドサーフィン uindosāfin
windsurfing

関連用語 kanrenyōgo • **vocabulary**

水上スキーヤー suijōsukīyā **waterskier**	**乗組員** norikumi'in **crew**	**風** kaze **wind**	**寄せ波** yosenami **surf**	**シート** shīto **sheet**	**センターボード** sentābōdo **centerboard**
サーファー sāfā **surfer**	**タッキングする** takkingu suru **tack (v)**	**波** nami **wave**	**急流** kyūryū **rapids**	**舵** kaji **rudder**	**転覆する** tempuku suru **capsize (v)**

乗馬 jōba • horseback riding

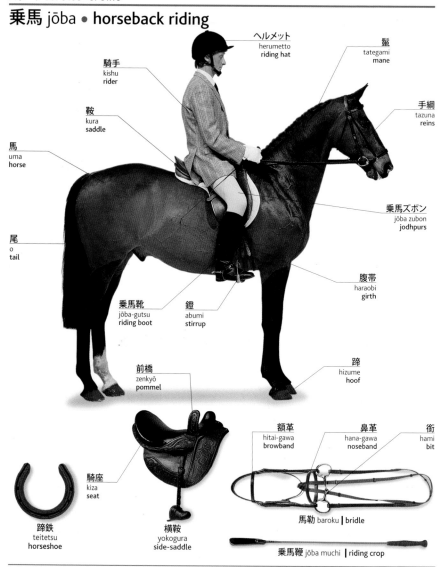

ヘルメット
herumetto
riding hat

鬣
tategami
mane

騎手
kishu
rider

手綱
tazuna
reins

鞍
kura
saddle

馬
uma
horse

乗馬ズボン
jōba zubon
jodhpurs

尾
o
tail

腹帯
haraobi
girth

乗馬靴
jōba-gutsu
riding boot

鐙
abumi
stirrup

蹄
hizume
hoof

前橋
zenkyō
pommel

額革
hitai-gawa
browband

鼻革
hana-gawa
noseband

衝
hami
bit

騎座
kiza
seat

蹄鉄
teitetsu
horseshoe

横鞍
yokogura
side-saddle

馬勒 baroku | **bridle**

乗馬鞭 jōba muchi | **riding crop**

競技 kyōgi • events

競走馬
kyōsōba
racehorse

障害物
shōgaibutsu
fence

競馬
keiba
horse race

障害競走
shōgai kyōsō
steeplechase

繋駕競走
keiga kyōsō
harness race

ロデオ
rodeo
rodeo

障害飛越
shōgai hietsu
showjumping

馬車レース
basha rēsu
carriage race

トレッキング torekkingu | trekking

馬場馬術 baba bajutsu | dressage

ポロ poro | polo

関連用語 kanrenyōgo • vocabulary

常歩 namiashi walk	駆歩 kakeashi canter	ジャンプ jampu jump	端綱 hazuna halter	パドック padokku paddock	平地競走 heichi kyōsō flat race
速歩 haya'ashi trot	襲歩 shūho gallop	馬手 umate groom	馬屋 umaya stable	アリーナ arīna arena	競馬場 keibajō racecourse

釣り tsuri • fishing

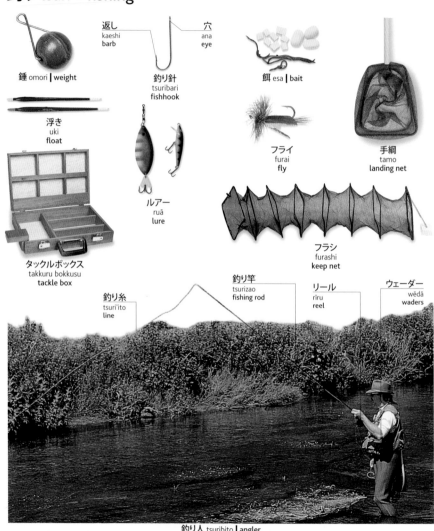

錘 omori | weight

返し
kaeshi
barb

穴
ana
eye

釣り針
tsuribari
fishhook

餌 esa | bait

浮き
uki
float

フライ
furai
fly

手綱
tamo
landing net

ルアー
ruā
lure

タックルボックス
takkuru bokkusu
tackle box

フラシ
furashi
keep net

釣り糸
tsuri'ito
line

釣り竿
tsurizao
fishing rod

リール
rīru
reel

ウェーダー
wēdā
waders

釣り人 tsuribito | angler

釣りの種類 tsuri no shurui ● types of fishing

淡水釣り
tansui-zuri
freshwater fishing

フライフィッシング
furai fisshingu
fly fishing

スポーツフィッシング
supōtsu fisshingu
sport fishing

深海釣り
shinkai-zuri
deep sea fishing

磯釣り
isozuri
surfcasting

動作 dōsa ● activities

投げる
nageru
cast (v)

釣る
tsuru
catch (v)

引き寄せる
hikiyoseru
reel in (v)

網打ちする
amiuchi suru
net (v)

放す
hanasu
release (v)

関連用語 kanrenyōgo ● vocabulary

誘き寄せる obikiyoseru **bait (v)**	**タックル** takkuru **tackle**	**雨具** amagu **waterproofs**	**釣り許可証** tsuri kyokashō **fishing permit**	**魚籠** biku **creel**
針にかかる hari ni kakaru **bite (v)**	**スプール** supūru **spool**	**竿** sao **pole**	**海釣り** umizuri **marine fishing**	**ヤス漁** yasu ryō **spearfishing**

スキー sukī ● skiing

スキー場
sukī-jō
ski slope

リフト
rifuto
chairlift

ケーブルカー
kēburu kā
cable car

スキーウェア
sukīwea
ski suit

ストック
sutokku
ski pole

グローブ
gurōbu
glove

ゲレンデ
gerende
ski run

スキー靴
sukī-gutsu
ski boot

安全柵
anzen saku
safety barrier

スキー板
sukī ita
ski

エッジ
ejji
edge

スキーヤー
sukīyā
skier

トップ
toppu
tip

競技 kyōgi • events

滑降
kakkō
downhill skiing

旗門
kimon
gate

回転
kaiten
slalom

ジャンプ
jampu
ski jump

クロスカントリー
kurosu-kantorī
cross-country skiing

ウィンタースポーツ wintā supōtsu • winter sports

アイスクライミング
aisu kuraimingu
ice climbing

アイススケート
aisu sukēto
ice skating

ゴーグル
gōguru
goggles

スケート靴
sukēto-gutsu
skate

フィギュアスケート
figyuasukēto
figure skating

スノーボード
sunōbōdo
snowboarding

ボブスレー
bobusurē
bobsled

リュージュ
ryūju
luge

スノーモービル
sunōmōbiru
snowmobile

そり滑り
sori suberi
sledding

関連 用語 kanrenyōgo • vocabulary

アルペンスキー arupen sukī **alpine skiing**	犬ぞり滑り inu-zori suberi **dog sledding**
大回転 daikaiten **giant slalom**	スピードスケート supīdo sukēto **speed skating**
ゲレンデ外 gerende-gai **off-piste**	バイアスロン baiasuron **biathlon**
カーリング kāringu **curling**	雪崩 nadare **avalanche**

他のスポーツ ta no supōtsu・**other sports**

グライダー
guraidā
glider

ハンググライダー
hangu guraidā
hang-glider

グライディング
guraidingu
gliding

パラシュート
parashūto
parachute

ハンググライディング
hangu guraidingu
hang-gliding

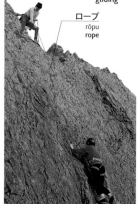

ロープ
rōpu
rope

ロッククライミング
rokku kuraimingu
rock climbing

パラシュート降下
parashūto kōka
parachuting

パラグライディング
paraguraidingu
paragliding

スカイダイビング
sukaidaibingu
skydiving

アブザイレン
abuzairen
rappelling

バンジージャンプ
banjī jampu
bungee jumping

ラリー
rarī
rally driving

自動車レース
jidōsha rēsu
auto racing

レーサー
rēsā
racing driver

モトクロス
motokurosu
motorcross

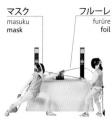

オートバイレース
ōtobai rēsu
motorcycle racing

スケートボード
sukētobōdo
skateboard

ローラースケート靴
rōrāsukēto-gutsu
rollerskate

スケートボード乗り
sukētobōdo-nori
skateboarding

ローラースケート
rōrāsukēto
roller skating

スティック
sutikku
stick

ラクロス
rakurosu
lacrosse

マスク
masuku
mask

フルーレ
furūre
foil

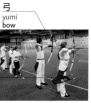

フェンシング
fenshingu
fencing

ピン
pin
pin

弓
yumi
bow

的
mato
target

矢
ya
arrow

矢筒
yazutsu
quiver

洋弓
yōkyū
archery

ターゲット射撃
tāgetto shageki
target shooting

ボール
bōru
bowling ball

ボウリング
bo'uringu
bowling

プール
pūru
pool

スヌーカー
sunūkā
snooker

フィットネス fittonesu・**fitness**

エアロバイク
earobaiku
exercise bike

フィットネス器具
fittonesu kigu
gym machine

ベンチ
benchi
bench

フリーウェイト
furī weito
free weights

バー
bā
bar

スポーツジム
supōtsu jimu
gym

ローイングマシーン
rōingu mashīn
rowing machine

トレッドミル
toreddomiru
treadmill

クロストレーナー
kurosu torēnā
cross trainer

パーソナルトレーナー
pāsonaru torēnā
personal trainer

ステッパー
suteppā
step machine

プール
pūru
swimming pool

サウナ
sauna
sauna

運動 undō • exercises

タイツ
taitsu
tights

ストレッチ
sutoretchi
stretch

ランジ
ranji
lunge

腕立て伏せ
udetatefuse
push-up

ダンベル
danberu
dumb bell

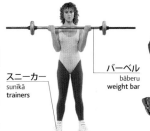

スクワット
sukuwatto
squat

腹筋運動
fukkin undō
sit-up

アームカール
āmu kāru
bicep curl

レッグプレス
reggu puresu
leg press

スニーカー
sunīkā
trainers

バーベル
bāberu
weight bar

ランニングシャツ
ranningu shatsu
vest

チェストプレス
chesuto puresu
chest press

ウェイトトレーニング
weito torēningu
weight training

ジョギング
jogingu
jogging

エアロビクス
earobikusu
aerobics

関連用語 kanrenyōgo • vocabulary

トレーニングする torēningu suru **train (v)**	その場でジョギングする sono ba de jogingu suru **run in place (v)**	伸ばす nobasu **extend (v)**	ピラティス piratisu **Pilates**	サーキットトレーニング sākitto torēningu **circuit training**
準備運動をする jumbi undō o suru **warm up (v)**	動かす ugokasu **flex (v)**	懸垂する kensui suru **pull up (v)**	ボクササイズ bokusasaizu **boxercise**	縄跳び nawatobi **skipping**

娯楽 goraku
leisure

劇場 gekijō • theater

幕
maku
curtain

袖
sode
wings

セット
setto
set

観客
kankyaku
audience

オーケストラ
ōkesutora
orchestra

舞台 butai | stage

座席
zaseki
seat

列
retsu
row

3階席
sangai seki
upper circle

ボックス席
bokkusu seki
box

バルコニー席
barukonī seki
balcony

2階席
nikai seki
circle

通路
tsūro
aisle

1階席
ikkai seki
stalls

座席配置 zaseki haichi | seating

関連用語 kanrenyōgo • vocabulary

配役
haiyaku
cast

台本
daihon
script

初日
shonichi
first night

俳優
haiyū
actor

背景
haikei
backdrop

休憩時間
kyūkei jikan
interval

女優
joyū
actress

監督
kantoku
director

プログラム
puroguramu
program

劇
geki
play

プロデューサー
purodyūsā
producer

オーケストラピット
ōkesutora pitto
orchestra pit

音楽会 ongakukai | concert

ミュージカル myūjikaru | musical

衣装
ishō
costume

バレエ barē | ballet

関連用語 kanrenyōgo • vocabulary

案内係
annai-gakari
usher

クラシック音楽
kurashikku ongaku
classical music

楽譜
gakufu
musical score

サウンドトラック
saundotorakku
soundtrack

拍手する
hakushu suru
applaud (v)

アンコール
ankōru
encore

今晩のチケットを2枚ください。
konban no chiketto o ni-mai kudasai.
I'd like two tickets for tonight's
performance.

何時に始まりますか。
nanji ni hajimarimasuka?
What time does it start?

オペラ opera | opera

映画 eiga • cinema

ポップコーン
poppukōn
popcorn

チケット売場
chiketto uriba
box office

ポスター
posutā
poster

ロビー
robī
lobby

映画館
eigakan
cinema hall

映写幕
eishamaku
screen

関連用語 kanrenyōgo • vocabulary

コメディ
komedi
comedy

スリラー
surirā
thriller

ホラー映画
horā eiga
horror movie

西部劇
seibugeki
western

恋愛物語
ren'ai monogatari
romance

SF映画
esu-efu eiga
science fiction movie

冒険
bōken
adventure

アニメ映画
anime eiga
animated movie

オーケストラ ōkesutora • orchestra

弦楽器 gengakki • strings

ハープ
hāpu
harp

指揮者
shikisha
conductor

コントラバス
kontorabasu
double bass

バイオリン
baiorin
violin

指揮台
shiki dai
podium

ビオラ
biora
viola

チェロ
chero
cello

楽譜
gakufu
score

ト音記号
to'on kigō
treble clef

音符
ompu
note

五線譜
gosenfu
staff

ヘ音記号
heon kigō
bass clef

記譜法 kifuhō **| notation**

ピアノ piano **| piano**

関連用語 kanrenyōgo • **vocabulary**

序曲 jokyoku **overture**	ソナタ sonata **sonata**	休止符 kyūshifu **rest**	シャープ shāpu **sharp**	本位記号 hon'i kigō **natural**	音階 onkai **scale**
交響曲 kōkyōkyoku **symphony**	楽器 gakki **instruments**	ピッチ pitchi **pitch**	フラット furatto **flat**	小節 shōsetsu **bar**	指揮棒 shikibō **baton**

木管楽器 mokkan gakki • **woodwind**

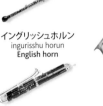

ピッコロ
pikkoro
piccolo

フルート
furūto
flute

オーボエ
ōboe
oboe

イングリッシュホルン
ingurisshu horun
English horn

クラリネット
kurarinetto
clarinet

バスクラリネット
basu kurarinetto
bass clarinet

ファゴット
fagotto
bassoon

コントラファゴット
kontora fagotto
double bassoon

サクソフォン
sakusofon
saxophone

打楽器 dagakki • **percussion**

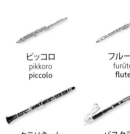

ボンゴ
bongo
bongos

スネアドラム
sunea doramu
snare drum

ケトルドラム
ketorudoramu
kettledrum

銅鑼
dora
gong

シンバル
shimbaru
cymbals

タンバリン
tambarin
tambourine

ビブラフォン
biburafon
vibraphone

トライアングル
toraianguru
triangle

マラカス
marakasu
maracas

金管楽器 kinkan gakki • **brass**

トランペット
torampetto
trumpet

トロンボーン
toronbōn
trombone

フレンチホルン
furenchi horun
French horn

チューバ
chūba
tuba

コンサート konsāto • concert

マイク
maiku
microphone

リードシンガー
rīdo shingā
lead singer

ドラマー
doramā
drummer

ギタリスト
gitarisuto
guitarist

ファン
fan
fans

ベーシスト
bēshisuto
bass guitarist

スピーカー
supīkā
speaker

ロックコンサート rokku konsāto | rock concert

楽器 gakki • instruments

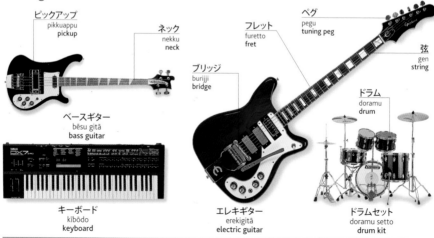

ピックアップ
pikkuappu
pickup

ネック
nekku
neck

フレット
furetto
fret

ペグ
pegu
tuning peg

弦
gen
string

ブリッジ
burijji
bridge

ドラム
doramu
drum

ベースギター
bēsu gitā
bass guitar

キーボード
kībōdo
keyboard

エレキギター
erekigitā
electric guitar

ドラムセット
doramu setto
drum kit

音楽ジャンル ongaku janru • music styles

ジャズ jazu | jazz

ブルース burūsu | blues

パンク panku | punk

フォーク fōku | folk music

ポップス poppusu | pop

ダンス dansu | dance

ラップ rappu | rap

ヘビーメタル hebī metaru
heavy metal

クラシック kurasshikku
classical music

関連用語 kanrenyōgo • vocabulary

歌	歌詞	メロディー	ビート	レゲエ	カントリー	スポットライト
uta	kashi	merodī	bīto	rege'e	kantorī	supottoraito
song	lyrics	melody	beat	reggae	country	spotlight

観光 kankō ● sightseeing

観光客
kankō kyaku
tourist

観光ルート
kankō rūto
itinerary

オープントップ
ōpun toppu
open top

観光バス kankō basu | tour bus

観光名所 kankō meisho | tourist attraction

観光ガイド
kankō gaido
tour guide

ガイド付きツアー
gaido-tsuki tsuā
guided tour

小像
shōzō
statuette

土産物
miyagemono
souvenirs

関連用語 kanrenyōgo ● vocabulary

開館 kaikan open	観光案内書 kankō annaisho guide book	カムコーダー kamukōdā camcorder	左 hidari left	…は、どこですか。 … wa doko desuka? Where is…?
閉館 heikan closed	フィルム firumu movie	カメラ kamera camera	右 migi right	道に迷ってしまいました。 michi ni mayotte shimaimashita. I'm lost.
入場料 nyūjō-ryō entrance fee	電池 denchi batteries	行き方 ikikata directions	まっすぐ massugu straight ahead	…への行き方を教えてください。 … e no ikikata o oshiete kudasai. Can you tell me the way to…?

名所 meisho • attractions

絵画
kaiga
painting

展示品
tenji-hin
exhibit

展覧会
tenrankai
exhibition

旧跡
kyūseki
famous ruin

美術館
bijutsukan
art gallery

記念碑
kinenhi
monument

博物館
hakubutsukan
museum

歴史的建造物
rekishi-teki kenzōbutsu
historic building

カジノ
kajino
casino

庭園
teien
gardens

国立公園
kokuritsu kōen
national park

案内 annai • information

時間
jikan
times

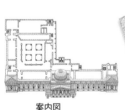

案内図
annai zu
floor plan

地図
chizu
map

時刻表
jikokuhyō
timetable

観光案内所
kankō annai-jo
tourist information

野外活動 yagai katsudō • outdoor activities

歩道
hodō
footpath

日時計
hidokei
sundial

カフェ
kafe
café

公園 kōen | park

芝生
shibafu
grass

ベンチ
benchi
bench

平面幾何学式庭園
heimen kikagaku-shiki teien
formal gardens

ジェットコースター
jetto kōsutā
roller coaster

遊園地
yūenchi
fairground

テーマパーク
tēma pāku
theme park

サファリパーク
safari pāku
safari park

動物園
dōbutsuen
zoo

活動 katsudō • activities

サイクリング
saikuringu
bicycling

ジョギング
jogingu
jogging

スケートボード
sukētobōdo
skateboarding

ローラーブレード
rōrāburēdo
rollerblading

乗馬道
jōba-dō
bridle path

野鳥観察
yachō kansatsu
bird watching

乗馬
jōba
horseback riding

ハイキング
haikingu
hiking

バスケット
basuketto
hamper

ピクニック
pikunikku
picnic

遊び場 asobiba • playground

砂場
sunaba
sandpit

水浴びプール
mizuabi pūru
paddling pool

ブランコ
buranko
swings

シーソー shīsō | **seesaw**

滑り台 suberidai | **slide**

ジャングルジム janguru jimu
climbing frame

海辺 umibe • beach

ホテル
hoteru
hotel

ビーチパラソル
bīchi parasoru
beach umbrella

海の家
umi no ie
beach hut

砂
suna
sand

波
nami
wave

海
umi
sea

ビーチバッグ
bīchi baggu
beach bag

ビキニ
bikini
bikini

日光浴をする nikkōyoku o suru | sunbathe (v)

監視員
kanshi'in
lifeguard

監視塔
kanshitō
lifeguard tower

防風フェンス
bōfū fensu
windbreak

遊歩道
yūhodō
promenade

デッキチェア
dekki chea
deck chair

サングラス
sangurasu
sunglasses

日除け帽
hiyoke-bō
sun hat

日焼けローション
hiyake rōshon
suntan lotion

日焼け止め
hiyakedome
sunblock

ビーチボール
bīchi bōru
beach ball

浮き輪
ukiwa
rubber ring

水着
mizugi
swimsuit

シャベル
shaberu
shovel

バケツ
baketsu
bucket

ビーチタオル
bīchi taoru
beach towel

砂の城
suna no shiro
sandcastle

貝殻
kaigara
shell

キャンプ kyampu • **camping**

トイレ
toire
toilets

ゴミ置場
gomi okiba
waste disposal

シャワー棟
shawā tō
shower block

電源装置
dengen sōchi
electric hook-up

フライシート
furaishīto
flysheet

ペグ
pegu
tent peg

ロープ
rōpu
guy rope

キャンピングトレーラー
kyampingu torērā
camper

キャンプ場 kyampujō | **campsite**

関連用語 kanrenyōgo • **vocabulary**

キャンプする
kyampu suru
camp (v)

管理事務所
kanri jimusho
site manager's office

空きサイトあり
aki saito ari
pitches available

空きなし
aki nashi
full

サイト
saito
pitch

テントを張る
tento o haru
pitch a tent (v)

ポール
pōru
tent pole

キャンプベッド
kyampu beddo
camp bed

ピクニックベンチ
pikunikku benchi
picnic bench

ハンモック
hammokku
hammock

キャンピングカー
kyampingu kā
camper van

トレーラー
torērā
trailer

炭
sumi
charcoal

着火剤
chakka-zai
firelighter

火をつける
hi o tsukeru
light a fire (v)

キャンプファイヤー
kyampufaiyā
campfire

グランドシート
gurando shīto
ground sheet

フレーム
furēmu
frame

魔法瓶
mahōbin
vacuum flask

リュックサック
ryukkusakku
backpack

水筒
suitō
water bottle

テント
tento
tent

蚊帳
kaya
mosquito net

虫除け
mushiyoke
insect repellent

懐中電灯
kaichūdentō
flashlight

保温ウエア
ho'on uea
thermals

ハイキングブーツ
haikingu būtsu
hiking boots

雨具
amagu
rain slickers

寝袋
nebukuro
sleeping bag

マット
matto
sleeping mat

ガスコンロ
gasu konro
camping stove

バーベキュー
bābekyū
barbecue

エアーマットレス eā mattoresu | air mattress

娯楽家電 goraku kaden • **home entertainment**

ポータブルCDプレーヤー
pōtaburu shī-dī purēyā
personal CD player

ミニディスクレコーダー
mini disuku rekōdā
mini disk recorder

MP3プレーヤー
emu-pī-surī purēyā
MP3 player

DVDディスク
dī-bui-dī disuku
DVD disk

DVDプレーヤー
dī-bui-dī purēyā
DVD player

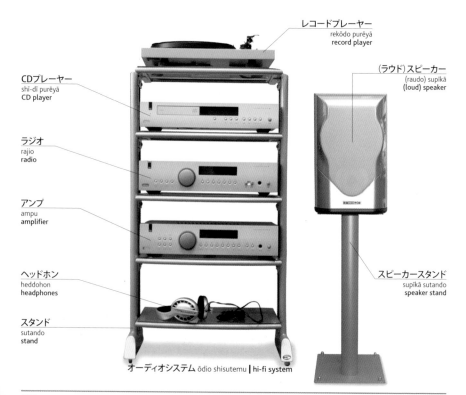

レコードプレーヤー
rekōdo purēyā
record player

CDプレーヤー
shī-dī purēyā
CD player

ラジオ
rajio
radio

アンプ
ampu
amplifier

ヘッドホン
heddohon
headphones

スタンド
sutando
stand

（ラウド）スピーカー
(raudo) supīkā
(loud) speaker

スピーカースタンド
supīkā sutando
speaker stand

オーディオシステム ōdio shisutemu | **hi-fi system**

ビデオテープ
bideo tēpu
video tape

画面
gamen
screen

アイカップ
aikappu
eyecup

ビデオレコーダー
bideo rekōdā
video recorder

カムコーダー
kamukōdā
camcorder

衛星アンテナ
eisei antena
satellite dish

ワイド画面テレビ
waido gamen terebi
widescreen television

コンソール
konsōru
console

早送り
hayaokuri
fast forward

一時停止
ichijiteishi
pause

録画
rokuga
record

音量
onryō
volume

コントローラー
kontorōrā
controller

巻き戻し
makimodoshi
rewind

再生
saisei
play

停止
teishi
stop

テレビゲーム terebi gēmu | **video game**

リモコン rimokon | **remote control**

関連用語 kanrenyōgo • vocabulary

コンパクトディスク kompakuto disuku **compact disk**	長編映画 chōhen eiga **feature film**	番組 bangumi **program**	有料チャンネル yūryō channeru **pay per view channel**	テレビを見る terebi o miru **watch television (v)**
カセットテープ kasetto tēpu **cassette tape**	コマーシャル komāsharu **advertisement**	ステレオ sutereo **stereo**	チャンネルを替える channeru o kaeru **change channel (v)**	テレビを消す terebi o kesu **turn the television off (v)**
カセットプレーヤー kasetto purēyā **cassette player**	ディジタル dijitaru **digital**	ケーブルテレビ kēburu terebi **cable television**	テレビを点ける terebi o tsukeru **turn the television on (v)**	ラジオをつける rajio o tsukeru **tune the radio (v)**

写真 shashin • photography

フィルムカウンター
firumu kauntā
frame counter

内蔵フラッシュ
naizō furasshu
flash

露出補正ダイヤル
roshutsu hosei daiyaru
aperture dial

シャッター
shattā
shutter release

フィルター
firutā
filter

レンズキャップ
renzu kyappu
lens cap

シャッター速度摘み
shattā sokudo tsumami
shutter-speed dial

レンズ
renzu
lens

一眼レフカメラ ichigan-refu kamera | **SLR camera**

フラッシュガン
furasshu gan
flash gun

露出計
roshutsukei
light meter

ズームレンズ
zūmu renzu
zoom lens

三脚
sankyaku
tripod

カメラの種類 kamera no shurui • types of camera

デジタルカメラ
dejitaru kamera
digital camera

APSカメラ
ē-pī-esu kamera
APS camera

インスタントカメラ
insutanto kamera
instant camera

使い捨てカメラ
tsukaisute kamera
disposable camera

写真撮影 shashin satsuei ● **photograph**

スプール
supūru
film spool

フィルム
firumu
film

ピントを合わせる
pinto o awaseru
focus (v)

現像する
genzō suru
develop (v)

ネガ
nega
negative

ランドスケープ
randosukēpu
landscape

ポートレート
pōtorēto
portrait

写真 shashin | **photograph**

アルバム
arubamu
photo album

写真用額縁
shashin-yō gakubuchi
photo frame

問題 mondai ● **problems**

露出不足
roshutsu-busoku
underexposed

露出オーバー
roshutsu-ōbā
overexposed

ピンぼけ
pimboke
out of focus

赤目
akame
red eye

関連用語 kanrenyōgo ● **vocabulary**

ファインダー faindā **viewfinder**	印画 inga **print**
カメラケース kamera kēsu **camera case**	無光沢 mukōtaku **matte**
露出 roshutsu **exposure**	光沢 kōtaku **gloss**
暗室 anshitsu **darkroom**	引き伸ばし hikinobashi **enlargement**
メモリカード memori kādo **memory card**	印画紙 ingashi **photo paper**

このフィルムを現像してください。
kono firumu o genzō shite kudasai.
I'd like this film processed.

ゲーム gēmu ● games

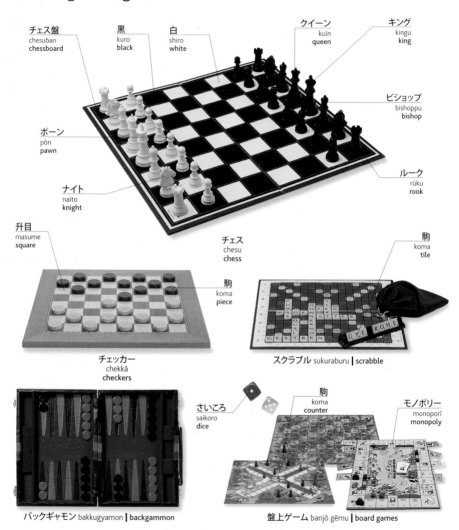

チェス盤
chesuban
chessboard

黒
kuro
black

白
shiro
white

クイーン
kuīn
queen

キング
kingu
king

ビショップ
bishoppu
bishop

ポーン
pōn
pawn

ルーク
rūku
rook

ナイト
naito
knight

升目
masume
square

チェス
chesu
chess

駒
koma
tile

駒
koma
piece

チェッカー
chekkā
checkers

スクラブル sukuraburu | scrabble

さいころ
saikoro
dice

駒
koma
counter

モノポリー
monoporī
monopoly

バックギャモン bakkugyamon | backgammon

盤上ゲーム banjō gēmu | board games

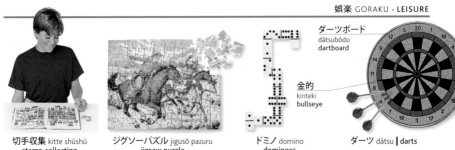

切手収集 kitte shūshū
stamp collecting

ジグソーパズル jigusō pazuru
jigsaw puzzle

ドミノ domino
dominoes

ダーツボード
dātsubōdo
dartboard

金的
kinteki
bullseye

ダーツ dātsu | darts

ジョーカー
jōkā
joker

ジャック
jakku
jack

クイーン
kuīn
queen

キング
kingu
king

エース
ēsu
ace

トランプ torampu | cards

ダイヤ
daiya
diamond

スペード
supēdo
spade

ハート
hāto
heart

クラブ
kurabu
club

切る kiru | shuffle (v)

配る kubaru | deal (v)

関連用語 kanrenyōgo • vocabulary

手 te move	勝つ katsu win (v)	敗者 haisha loser	点 ten point	ブリッジ burijji bridge	さいころを転がしてください。 saikoro o korogashite kudasai. Roll the dice.
遊ぶ asobu play (v)	勝者 shōsha winner	ゲーム gēmu game	得点 tokuten score	トランプ一組 torampu hito-kumi deck of cards	誰の番ですか。 dare no ban desuka? Whose turn is it?
プレーヤー purēyā player	負ける makeru lose (v)	賭け kake bet	ポーカー pōkā poker	スート sūto suit	貴方の番です。 anata no ban desu. It's your move.

美術と工芸1 bijutsu to kōgei • arts and crafts 1

画家
gaka
artist

絵
e
painting

イーゼル
īzeru
easel

キャンバス
kyambasu
canvas

絵筆
efude
brush

パレット
paretto
palette

図画 zuga | painting

絵具 enogu • paints

油絵具
abura enogu
oil paints

水彩絵具
suisai enogu
watercolor paint

パステル
pasuteru
pastels

アクリル絵具
akuriru enogu
acrylic paint

ポスターカラー posutā karā
poster paint

色 iro • colours

赤 aka | red

青 ao | blue

黄色 ki'iro
yellow

緑 midori | green

オレンジ色 orenji iro
orange

紫 murasaki
purple

白 shiro | white

黒 kuro | black

灰色 hai'iro | gray

ピンク pinku
pink

茶色 chairo | brown

藍色 ai'iro
indigo

他の工芸 ta no kōgei • other crafts

スケッチブック
suketchi bukku
sketch pad

スケッチ
suketchi
sketch

インク
inku
ink

鉛筆
empitsu
pencil

木炭
mokutan
charcoal

素描 sobyō | **drawing**

版画 hanga | **printing**

エッチング etchingu
engraving

石材
sekizai
stone

木槌
kizuchi
mallet

彫刻刀
chōkokutō
chisel

木材
mokuzai
wood

成形道具
seikei dōgu
modeling tool

ロクロ
rokuro
potter's wheel

彫刻
chōkoku
sculpting

木工
mokkō
woodworking

糊
nori
glue

厚紙
atsugami
cardboard

粘土
nendo
clay

コラージュ korāju | **collage**

陶芸 tōgei | **pottery**

ジュエリー制作
juerī seisaku
jewellery making

張子
hariko
papier-mâché

折り紙
origami
origami

模型制作
mokei seisaku
model making

美術と工芸2 bijutsu to kōgei • **arts and crafts 2**

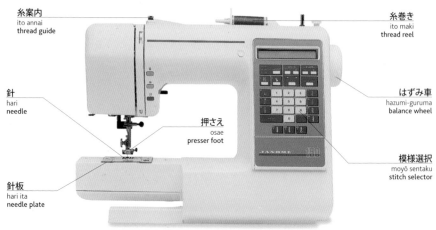

糸案内
ito annai
thread guide

糸巻き
ito maki
thread reel

針
hari
needle

はずみ車
hazumi-guruma
balance wheel

押さえ
osae
presser foot

針板
hari ita
needle plate

模様選択
moyō sentaku
stitch selector

ミシン mishin | **sewing machine**

鋏
hasami
scissors

型紙
katagami
pattern

針刺し
harisashi
pincushion

メジャー
mejā
tape measure

生地
kiji
material

待針
machibari
pin

裁縫箱 saihō-bako
sewing basket

糸
ito
thread

受け金
ukegane
eye

ボビン
bobin
bobbin

鉤ホック
kagi hokku
hook

指貫
yubinuki
thimble

チャコ
chako
tailor's chalk

ダミー
damī
tailor's dummy

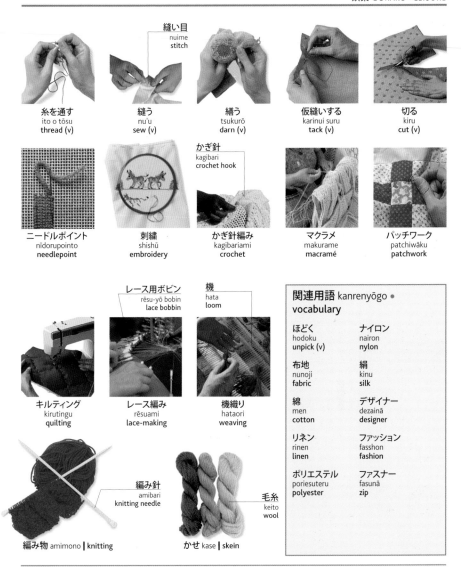

縫い目
nuime
stitch

糸を通す
ito o tōsu
thread (v)

縫う
nu'u
sew (v)

繕う
tsukurō
darn (v)

仮縫いする
karinui suru
tack (v)

切る
kiru
cut (v)

かぎ針
kagibari
crochet hook

ニードルポイント
nīdorupointo
needlepoint

刺繍
shishū
embroidery

かぎ針編み
kagibariami
crochet

マクラメ
makurame
macramé

パッチワーク
patchiwāku
patchwork

レース用ボビン
rēsu-yō bobin
lace bobbin

機
hata
loom

キルティング
kirutingu
quilting

レース編み
rēsuami
lace-making

機織り
hataori
weaving

編み針
amibari
knitting needle

編み物 amimono | **knitting**

毛糸
keito
wool

かせ kase | **skein**

関連用語 kanrenyōgo • vocabulary

ほどく
hodoku
unpick (v)

ナイロン
nairon
nylon

布地
nunoji
fabric

絹
kinu
silk

綿
men
cotton

デザイナー
dezainā
designer

リネン
rinen
linen

ファッション
fasshon
fashion

ポリエステル
poriesuteru
polyester

ファスナー
fasunā
zip

環境 kankyō
environment

宇宙空間 uchūkūkan • **space**

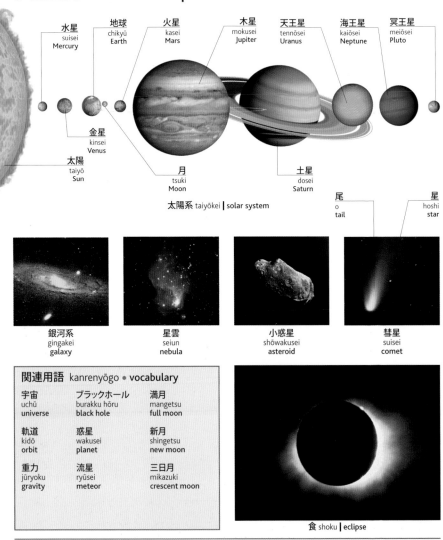

水星
suisei
Mercury

地球
chikyū
Earth

火星
kasei
Mars

木星
mokusei
Jupiter

天王星
tennōsei
Uranus

海王星
kaiōsei
Neptune

冥王星
meiōsei
Pluto

金星
kinsei
Venus

太陽
taiyō
Sun

月
tsuki
Moon

土星
dosei
Saturn

太陽系 taiyōkei | solar system

尾
o
tail

星
hoshi
star

銀河系
gingakei
galaxy

星雲
seiun
nebula

小惑星
shōwakusei
asteroid

彗星
suisei
comet

関連用語 kanrenyōgo • **vocabulary**

宇宙
uchū
universe

ブラックホール
burakku hōru
black hole

満月
mangetsu
full moon

軌道
kidō
orbit

惑星
wakusei
planet

新月
shingetsu
new moon

重力
jūryoku
gravity

流星
ryūsei
meteor

三日月
mikazuki
crescent moon

食 shoku | eclipse

宇宙探検 uchū tanken • space exploration

レーダー
rēdā
radar

スラスター
surasutā
thruster

スペースシャトル
supēsu shatoru
space shuttle

宇宙服
uchūfuku
space suit

乗船口
jōsen-guchi
crew hatch

ブースター
būsutā
booster

宇宙飛行士 uchūhikōshi
astronaut

月着陸船 tsukichakurikusen | lunar module

発射台
hasshadai
launch pad

発射
hassha
launch

人工衛星
jinkōeisei
satellite

宇宙ステーション
uchū sutēshon
space station

天文学 tenmongaku • astronomy

天体望遠鏡
tentaibōenkyō
telescope

三脚
sankyaku
tripod

星座
seiza
constellation

双眼鏡
sōgankyō
binoculars

地球 chikyū ● Earth

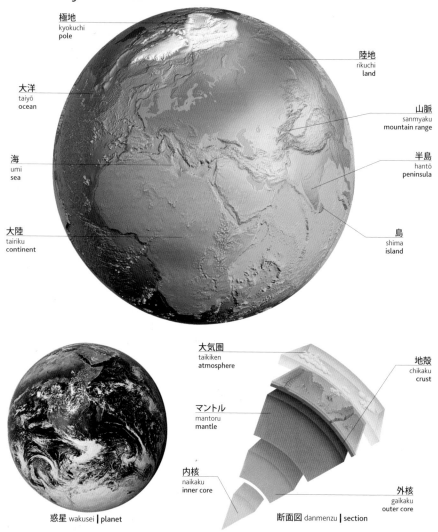

極地
kyokuchi
pole

陸地
rikuchi
land

大洋
taiyō
ocean

山脈
sanmyaku
mountain range

海
umi
sea

半島
hantō
peninsula

大陸
tairiku
continent

島
shima
island

大気圏
taikiken
atmosphere

地殻
chikaku
crust

マントル
mantoru
mantle

内核
naikaku
inner core

外核
gaikaku
outer core

惑星 wakusei | planet

断面図 danmenzu | section

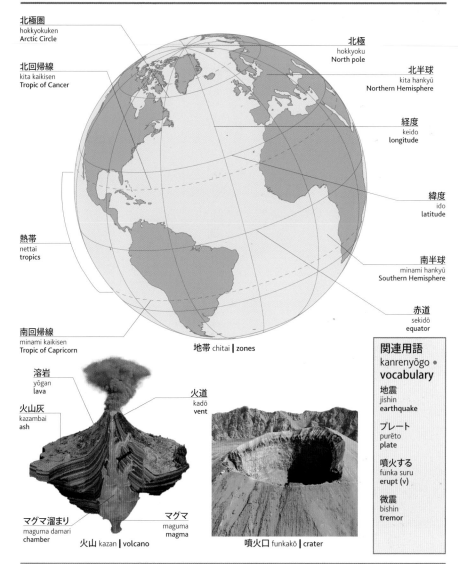

北極圏
hokkyokuken
Arctic Circle

北回帰線
kita kaikisen
Tropic of Cancer

北極
hokkyoku
North pole

北半球
kita hankyū
Northern Hemisphere

経度
keido
longitude

緯度
ido
latitude

熱帯
nettai
tropics

南半球
minami hankyū
Southern Hemisphere

赤道
sekidō
equator

南回帰線
minami kaikisen
Tropic of Capricorn

地帯 chitai | zones

溶岩
yōgan
lava

火道
kadō
vent

火山灰
kazambai
ash

マグマ溜まり
maguma damari
chamber

マグマ
maguma
magma

火山 kazan | volcano

噴火口 funkakō | crater

関連用語
kanrenyōgo •
vocabulary

地震
jishin
earthquake

プレート
purēto
plate

噴火する
funka suru
erupt (v)

微震
bishin
tremor

地勢 chisei · landscape

山
yama
mountain

斜面
shamen
slope

川岸
kawagishi
bank

川
kawa
river

急流
kyūryū
rapids

岩
iwa
rocks

氷河
hyōga
glacier

谷間 tanima | valley

丘陵
kyūryō
hill

台地
daichi
plateau

渓谷
keikoku
gorge

洞窟
dōkutsu
cave

平野 heiya | plain

砂漠 sabaku | desert

森林 shinrin | forest

林地 rinchi | wood

雨林
urin
rain forest

湿地
shitchi
swamp

草地
kusachi
meadow

草原
sōgen
grassland

滝
taki
waterfall

渓流
keiryū
stream

湖
mizu'umi
lake

間欠泉
kanketsusen
geyser

海岸
kaigan
coast

崖
gake
cliff

珊瑚礁
sangoshō
coral reef

河口
kakō
estuary

気象 kishō・weather

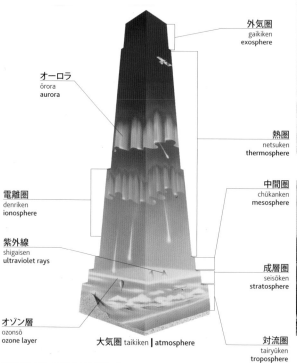

外気圏
gaikiken
exosphere

オーロラ
ōrora
aurora

熱圏
netsuken
thermosphere

晴天 seiten | sunshine

電離圏
denriken
ionosphere

中間圏
chūkanken
mesosphere

紫外線
shigaisen
ultraviolet rays

成層圏
seisōken
stratosphere

風 kaze | wind

オゾン層
ozonsō
ozone layer

大気圏 taikiken | atmosphere

対流圏
tairyūken
troposphere

関連用語 kanrenyōgo・vocabulary

霙 mizore sleet	晴れ hare sunny	寒い samui cold	雨がちな ame-gachi na wet	強風 kyōfū gale	暑い/寒いです。 atsui/samui desu. I'm hot/cold.
雹 hyō hail	曇り kumori cloudy	暖かい atatakai warm	湿気の多い shikke no ōi humid	気温 kion temperature	雨が降っています。 ame ga futte imasu. It's raining.
雷 kaminari thunder	暑い atsui hot	乾燥した kansō shita dry	風の強い kaze no tsuyoi windy	台風 taifū typhoon	... 度です。 ... do desu. It's ... degrees.

稲妻 inazuma lightning

雲 kumo | cloud

雨 ame | rain

嵐 arashi | storm

靄 moya | mist

霧 kiri | fog

虹 niji | rainbow

雪 yuki | snow

霜 shimo | frost

氷 kōri | ice

氷柱 tsurara icicle

氷結 hyōketsu | freeze

ハリケーン harikēn hurricane

旋風 tsumujikaze tornado

モンスーン monsūn monsoon

洪水 kōzui | flood

岩石 ganseki • rocks

火成岩 kaseigan • igneous

花崗岩
kakōgan
granite

黒曜石
kokuyōseki
obsidian

玄武岩
gembugan
basalt

軽石
karuishi
pumice

堆積岩 taisekigan • sedimentary

砂岩
sagan
sandstone

石灰岩
sekkaigan
limestone

白亜
hakua
chalk

燧石
suiseki
flint

礫岩
rekigan
conglomerate

石炭
sekitan
coal

変成岩 henseigan • metamorphic

粘板岩
nembangan
slate

片岩
hengan
schist

片麻岩
henmagan
gneiss

大理石
dairiseki
marble

宝石 hōseki • gems

ルビー
rubī
ruby

アメジスト
amejisuto
amethyst

ダイヤモンド
daiyamondo
diamond

ジェット
jetto
jet

オパール
opāru
opal

ムーンストーン
mūnsutōn
moonstone

ガーネット
gānetto
garnet

アクアマリン
akuamarin
aquamarine

翡翠
hisui
jade

エメラルド
emerarudo
emerald

サファイア
safaia
sapphire

トパーズ
topāzu
topaz

トルマリン
torumarin
tourmaline

鉱石 kōseki ● minerals

石英
sekiei
quartz

雲母
unmo
mica

硫黄
iō
sulfur

ヘマタイト
hemataito
hematite

方解石
hōkaiseki
calcite

孔雀石
kujakuseki
malachite

トルコ石
torukoishi
turquoise

縞瑪瑙
shimamenō
onyx

瑪瑙
menō
agate

黒鉛
kokuen
graphite

金属 kinzoku ● metals

金
kin
gold

銀
gin
silver

プラチナ
purachina
platinum

ニッケル
nikkeru
nickel

鉄
tetsu
iron

銅
dō
copper

錫
suzu
tin

アルミニウム
aruminiumu
aluminum

水銀
suigin
mercury

亜鉛
aen
zinc

動物1 dōbutsu • animals 1
哺乳類 honyūrui • mammals

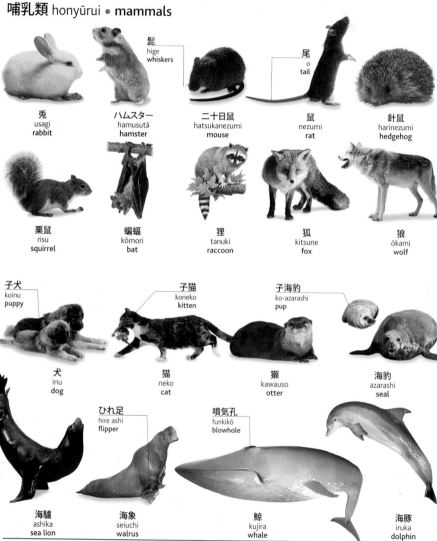

髭
hige
whiskers

尾
o
tail

兎
usagi
rabbit

ハムスター
hamusutā
hamster

二十日鼠
hatsukanezumi
mouse

鼠
nezumi
rat

針鼠
harinezumi
hedgehog

栗鼠
risu
squirrel

蝙蝠
kōmori
bat

狸
tanuki
raccoon

狐
kitsune
fox

狼
ōkami
wolf

子犬
koinu
puppy

子猫
koneko
kitten

子海豹
ko-azarashi
pup

犬
inu
dog

猫
neko
cat

獺
kawauso
otter

海豹
azarashi
seal

ひれ足
hire ashi
flipper

噴気孔
funkikō
blowhole

海驢
ashika
sea lion

海象
seiuchi
walrus

鯨
kujira
whale

海豚
iruka
dolphin

枝角
eda tsuno
antler

鬣
tategami
mane

こぶ
kobu
hump

蹄
hizume
hoof

鹿
shika
deer

縞馬
shimauma
zebra

麒麟
kirin
giraffe

駱駝
rakuda
camel

鼻
hana
trunk

牙
kiba
tusk

角
tsuno
horn

河馬
kaba
hippopotamus

象
zō
elephant

犀
sai
rhinoceros

虎
tora
tiger

鬣
tategami
mane

ライオン
raion
lion

猿
saru
monkey

ゴリラ
gorira
gorilla

コアラ
koara
koala

袋
fukuro
pouch

パンダ
panda
panda

爪
tsume
claw

カンガルー
kangarū
kangaroo

熊
kuma
bear

北極熊
hokkyokuguma
polar bear

動物2 dōbutsu ● animals 2

鳥類 chōrui ● birds

尾
o
tail

カナリヤ
kanariya
canary

雀
suzume
sparrow

蜂鳥
hachidori
hummingbird

燕
tsubame
swallow

烏
karasu
crow

鳩
hato
pigeon

啄木鳥
kitsutsuki
woodpecker

隼
hayabusa
falcon

梟
fukurō
owl

鴎
kamome
gull

鷲
washi
eagle

ペリカン
perikan
pelican

フラミンゴ
furamingo
flamingo

鸛
kōnotori
stork

鶴
tsuru
crane

ペンギン
pengin
penguin

駝鳥
dachō
ostrich

鵞鳥 gachō | goose

白鳥
hakuchō
swan

孔雀
kujaku
peacock

雉
kiji
pheasant

七面鳥
shichimenchō
turkey

嘴
kuchibashi
bill

鸚哥
inko
cockatoo

羽根
hane
feather

翼
tsubasa
wing

爪
tsume
claw

鸚鵡
ōmu
parrot

爬虫類 hachūrui · reptiles

鱗
uroko
scales

アリゲーター
arigētā
alligator

蜥蜴
tokage
lizard

イグアナ
iguana
iguana

甲羅
kōra
shell

亀
kame
turtle

陸亀
riku-game
tortoise

蛇
hebi
snake

鼻
hana
snout

クロコダイル
kurokodairu
crocodile

動物3 dōbutsu • animals 3

両生類 ryōseirui • amphibians

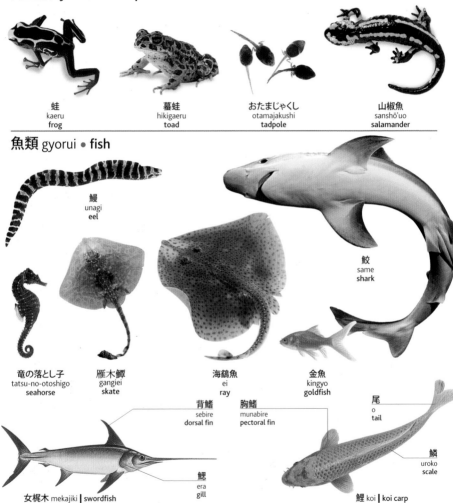

蛙
kaeru
frog

蟇蛙
hikigaeru
toad

おたまじゃくし
otamajakushi
tadpole

山椒魚
sanshō'uo
salamander

魚類 gyorui • fish

鰻
unagi
eel

鮫
same
shark

竜の落とし子
tatsu-no-otoshigo
seahorse

雁木鱏
gangiei
skate

海鷂魚
ei
ray

金魚
kingyo
goldfish

背鰭
sebire
dorsal fin

胸鰭
munabire
pectoral fin

尾
o
tail

鱗
uroko
scale

女梶木 mekajiki | **swordfish**

鰓
era
gill

鯉 koi | **koi carp**

無脊椎動物 musekitsui dōbutsu • invertebrates

蟻
ari
ant

白蟻
shiroari
termite

蜜蜂
mitsubachi
bee

蜂
hachi
wasp

kabutomushi
beetle

触角
shokkaku
antenna

ゴキブリ
gokiburi
cockroach

蛾
ga
moth

蝶
chō
butterfly

繭
mayu
cocoon

芋虫
imomushi
caterpillar

毒針
dokubari
sting

蟋蟀 kōrogi | **cricket**

蝗
inago
grasshopper

蟷螂
kamakiri
praying mantis

蠍
sasori
scorpion

mukade
centipede

蜻蛉
tombo
dragonfly

蠅
hae
fly

蚊
ka
mosquito

天道虫
tentōmushi
ladybug

蜘蛛
kumo
spider

蛞蝓
namekuji
slug

蝸牛
katatsumuri
snail

蚯蚓 mimizu | **worm**

海星
hitode
starfish

紫貽貝
murasaki igai
mussel

蟹 kani | **crab**

ロブスター robusutā
lobster

蛸 tako | **octopus**

烏賊 ika | **squid**

水母 kurage | **jellyfish**

植物 shokubutsu • plants

木 ki • tree

枝
eda
branch

葉
ha
leaf

小枝
koeda
twig

樹皮
juhi
bark

根
ne
root

幹
miki
trunk

樫 kashi | oak

柳
yanagi
willow

ポプラ
popura
poplar

ユーカリ
yūkari
eucalyptus

唐松
karamatsu
larch

ブナ
buna
beech

白樺
shirakaba
birch

松
matsu
pine

ヒマラヤ杉
himarayasugi
cedar

楓
kaede
maple

楡
nire
elm

リンデン
rinden
linden

実
mi
berry

柊
hi'iragi
holly

椰子
yashi
palm

296

顕花植物 kenkashokubutsu • flowering plant

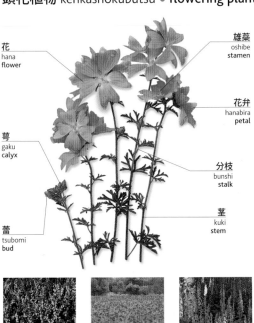

花
hana
flower

雄蘂
oshibe
stamen

花弁
hanabira
petal

萼
gaku
calyx

分枝
bunshi
stalk

茎
kuki
stem

蕾
tsubomi
bud

金鳳花
kimpōge
buttercup

雛菊
hinagiku
daisy

薊
azami
thistle

蒲公英
tampopo
dandelion

ヒース
hīsu
heather

芥子
keshi
poppy

狐の手袋
kitsune-no-tebukuro
foxglove

忍冬
suikazura
honeysuckle

向日葵
himawari
sunflower

クローバー
kurōbā
clover

釣鐘水仙
tsurigane suisen
bluebells

桜草
sakurasō
primrose

ルーピン
rūpin
lupins

刺草
irakusa
nettle

市街 shigai • town

通り
tōri
street

縁石
fuchi'ishi
curb

街角
machikado
street corner

商店
shōten
store

交差点
kōsaten
intersection

一方通行
ippōtsūkō
one-way street

歩道
hodō
pavement

オフィスビル
ofisu biru
office building

マンション
manshon
apartment
building

路地
roji
alley

駐車場
chūshajō
parking lot

道路標識
dōro hyōshiki
street sign

ボラード
borādo
traffic post

街灯
gaitō
street light

建物 tatemono • buildings

市庁舎
shichōsha
town hall

図書館
toshokan
library

映画館
eigakan
movie theater

劇場
gekijō
theater

大学
daigaku
university

学校
gakkō
school

摩天楼
matenrō
skyscraper

区域 kuiki • areas

工業団地
kōgyōdanchi
industrial complex

都市
toshi
city

郊外
kōgai
suburb

村
mura
village

関連用語 kanrenyōgo • vocabulary

歩行者天国 hokōsha-tengoku **pedestrian zone**	**脇道** wakimichi **side street**	**マンホール** manhōru **manhole**	**排水溝** haisuikō **gutter**	**教会** kyōkai **church**
大通り ōdōri **avenue**	**広場** hiroba **square**	**バス停** basutei **bus stop**	**工場** kōjō **factory**	**下水道** gesuidō **drain**

建築 kenchiku • architecture

建物と構造 tatemono to kōzō • buildings and structures

頂華
chōge
finial

小塔　尖塔
shōtō　sentō
turret　spire

濠
hori
moat

破風
hafu
gable

摩天楼
matenrō
skyscraper

城
shiro
castle

丸屋根
maruyane
dome

塔
tō
tower

教会
kyōkai
church

モスク
mosuku
mosque

アーチ形屋根
āchi-gata yane
vault

コーニス
kōnisu
cornice

寺院
ji'in
temple

シナゴーグ
shinagōgu
synagogue

柱
hashira
pillar

ダム
damu
dam

橋
hashi
bridge

大聖堂 daiseidō | cathedral

建築様式 kenchiku yōshiki · **styles**

ゴシック goshikku | **gothic**

アーキトレーブ
ākitorēbu
architrave

ルネサンス
runesansu
Renaissance

バロック
barokku
baroque

聖歌隊席
seikatai seki
choir

ロココ
rokoko
rococo

アーチ
āchi
arch

フリーズ
furīzu
frieze

ペディメント
pedimento
pediment

控え壁
hikaekabe
buttress

新古典主義
shinkotenshugi
neoclassical

アールヌーボー
āru nūbō
art nouveau

アールデコ
āru deko
art deco

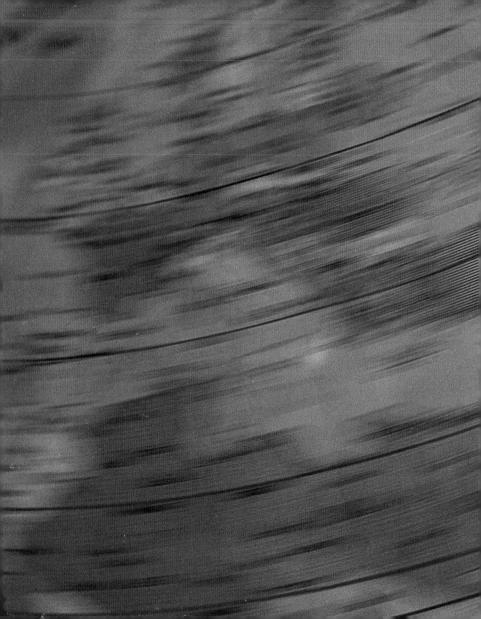

参考資料 sankō shiryō
reference

時間 jikan • time

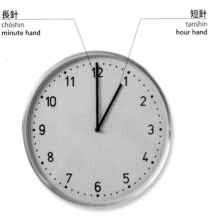

長針
chōshin
minute hand

短針
tanshin
hour hand

時計
tokei
clock

関連用語 kanrenyōgo • vocabulary

秒 byō second	現在 genzai now	15分 jūgo-fun a quarter of an hour
分 fun minute	後 nochi later	20分 nijuppun twenty minutes
時 ji hour	30分 sanjuppun half an hour	40分 yonjuppun forty minutes

今、何時ですか。
ima nanji desuka?
What time is it?

3時です。
san-ji desu.
It's three o'clock.

1時5分
ichi-ji go-fun
five past one

1時10分
ichi-ji juppun
ten past one

1時15分
ichi-ji jūgo-fun
quarter past one

1時20分
ichi-ji nijuppun
twenty past one

秒針
byōshin
second hand

1時25分
ichi-ji nijūgo-fun
twenty five past one

1時半
ichi-ji han
one thirty

1時35分
ichi-ji sanjūgo-fun
twenty five to two

1時40分前
ichi-ji yonjuppun
twenty to two

2時15分前
ni-ji jūgo-fun mae
quarter to two

2時10分前
ni-ji juppun mae
ten to two

2時5分前
ni-ji go-fun mae
five to two

2時
ni-ji
two o'clock

日中と夜 nitchū to yoru · **night and day**

真夜中 mayonaka | midnight

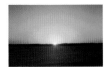
日の出 hinode | sunrise

夜明け yoake | dawn

朝 asa | morning

日没
nichibotsu
sunset

正午
shōgo
midday

夕暮れ yūgure | dusk

晩 ban | evening

午後 gogo | afternoon

関連用語 kanrenyōgo · **vocabulary**

早い
hayai
early

早いですね。
hayai desune.
You're early.

時間通りに来てください。
jikan-dōri ni kite kudasai.
Please be on time.

何時に終わりますか。
nanji ni owarimasuka?
What time does it finish?

時間通り
jikan-dōri
on time

遅刻です。
chikoku desu.
You're late.

また後で。
mata ato de.
I'll see you later.

遅くなってきました。
osokunatte kimashita.
It's getting late.

遅い
osoi
late

もうすぐ到着します。
mōsugu tōchaku shimasu.
I'll be there soon.

何時に始まりますか。
nanji ni hajimarimasuka?
What time does it start?

時間は、どのくらいかかりますか。
jikan wa donokurai kakarimasuka?
How long will it last?

カレンダー karendā • **calendar**

月
tsuki
month

年
toshi
year

一月
ichigatsu
January

2010

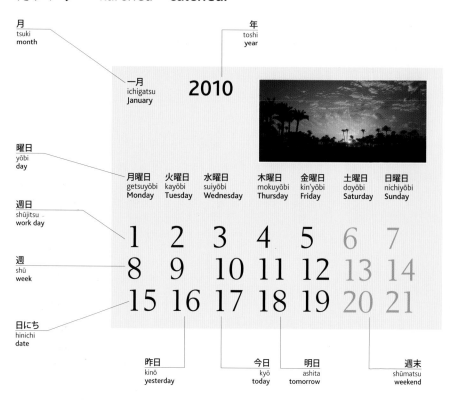

曜日
yōbi
day

週日
shūjitsu
work day

週
shū
week

日にち
hinichi
date

月曜日 getsuyōbi **Monday**	火曜日 kayōbi **Tuesday**	水曜日 suiyōbi **Wednesday**	木曜日 mokuyōbi **Thursday**	金曜日 kin'yōbi **Friday**	土曜日 doyōbi **Saturday**	日曜日 nichiyōbi **Sunday**
1	2	3	4	5	6	7
8	9	10	11	12	13	14
15	16	17	18	19	20	21

昨日
kinō
yesterday

今日
kyō
today

明日
ashita
tomorrow

週末
shūmatsu
weekend

関連用語 kanrenyōgo • **vocabulary**

一月 ichigatsu **January**	三月 sangatsu **March**	五月 gogatsu **May**	七月 shichigatsu **July**	九月 kugatsu **September**	十一月 jūichigatsu **November**
二月 nigatsu **February**	四月 shigatsu **April**	六月 rokugatsu **June**	八月 hachigatsu **August**	十月 jūgatsu **October**	十二月 jūnigatsu **December**

年 toshi • years

1900 一九〇〇年 sen kyūhyaku nen • nineteen hundred

1901 一九〇一年 sen kyūhyaku ichi nen • nineteen hundred and one

1910 一九一〇年 sen kyūhyaku jū nen • nineteen ten

2000 二〇〇〇年 nisen nen • two thousand

2001 二〇〇一年 nisen ichi nen • two thousand and one

季節 kisetsu • seasons

春
haru
spring

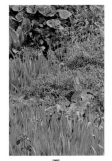

夏
natsu
summer

秋
aki
autumn

冬
fuyu
winter

関連用語 kanrenyōgo • vocabulary

世紀 seiki century	今週 konshū this week	明後日 asatte the day after tomorrow	今日は何日ですか。 kyō wa nannichi desuka? What's the date today?
十年間 jūnenkan decade	先週 senshū last week	毎週 maishū weekly	2002年2月17日です。 nisen ni nen nigatsu jūshichi nichi desu. It's February seventeenth, two thousand and two.
千年間 sennenkan millennium	来週 raishū next week	毎月 maitsuki monthly	
二週間 nishūkan fortnight	一昨日 ototoi the day before yesterday	毎年 maitoshi annual	

数字 sūji · numbers

0	零 rei · zero		20	二十 nijū · twenty
1	一 ichi · one		21	二十一 nijūichi · twenty-one
2	二 ni · two		22	二十二 nijūni · twenty-two
3	三 san · three		30	三十 sanjū · thirty
4	四 shi/yon · four		40	四十 shijū/yonjū · forty
5	五 go · five		50	五十 gojū · fifty
6	六 roku · six		60	六十 rokujū · sixty
7	七 shichi/nana · seven		70	七十 shichijū/nanajū · seventy
8	八 hachi · eight		80	八十 hachijū · eighty
9	九 ku/kyū · nine		90	九十 kyūjū · ninety
10	十 jū · ten		100	百 hyaku · one hundred
11	十一 jūichi · eleven		110	百十 hyakujū · one hundred and ten
12	十二 jūni · twelve		200	二百 nihyaku · two hundred
13	十三 jūsan · thirteen		300	三百 sambyaku · three hundred
14	十四 jūshi/jūyon · fourteen		400	四百 yonhyaku · four hundred
15	十五 jūgo · fifteen		500	五百 gohyaku · five hundred
16	十六 jūroku · sixteen		600	六百 roppyaku · six hundred
17	十七 jūshichi/jūnana · seventeen		700	七百 nanahyaku · seven hundred
18	十八 jūhachi · eighteen		800	八百 happyaku · eight hundred
19	十九 jūku/jūkyū · nineteen		900	九百 kyūhyaku · nine hundred

1,000 千 sen • **one thousand**

10,000 一万 ichiman • **ten thousand**

20,000 二万 niman • **twenty thousand**

50,000 五万 goman • **fifty thousand**

55,500 五万五千五百 goman gosen gohyaku • **fifty-five thousand five hundred**

100,000 十万 jūman • **one hundred thousand**

1,000,000 百万 hyakuman • **one million**

1,000,000,000 十億 jūoku • **one billion**

一番目 ichi banme first

二番目 ni banme second

三番目 san banme third

四番目 yon banme • **fourth**

五番目 go banme • **fifth**

六番目 roku banme • **sixth**

七番目 nana banme • **seventh**

八番目 hachi banme • **eighth**

九番目 kyū banme • **ninth**

十番目 jū banme • **tenth**

十一番目 jūichi banme • **eleventh**

十二番目 jūni banme • **twelfth**

十三番目 jūsan banme • **thirteenth**

十四番目 jūyon banme • **fourteenth**

十五番目 jūgo banme • **fifteenth**

十六番目 jūroku banme • **sixteenth**

十七番目 jūnana banme • **seventeenth**

十八番目 jūhachi banme • **eighteenth**

十九番目 jūkyū banme • **nineteenth**

二十番目 nijū banme • **twentieth**

二十一番目 nijūichi banme • **twenty-first**

二十二番目 nijūni banme • **twenty-second**

二十三番目 nijūsan banme • **twenty-third**

三十番目 sanjū banme • **thirtieth**

四十番目 yonjū banme • **fortieth**

五十番目 gojū banme • **fiftieth**

六十番目 rokujū banme • **sixtieth**

七十番目 nanajū banme • **seventieth**

八十番目 hachijū banme • **eightieth**

九十番目 kyūjū banme • **ninetieth**

百番目 hyaku banme • **one hundredth**

計量 keiryō • weights and measures

面積 menseki • area

平方フィート
heihō fito
square foot

平方メートル
heihō mētoru
square meter

距離 kyori • distance

キロメートル
kiromētoru
kilometer

マイル
mairu
mile

上皿
uwazara
pan

キログラム
kiroguramu
kilogram

グラム
guramu
gram

ポンド
pondo
pound

オンス
onsu
ounce

秤 hakari | scales

関連用語 kanrenyōgo • vocabulary

ヤード yādo **yard**	トン ton **ton**	測る hakaru **measure (v)**
メートル mētoru **meter**	ミリグラム miriguramu **milligram**	量る hakaru **weigh (v)**

長さ nagasa • length

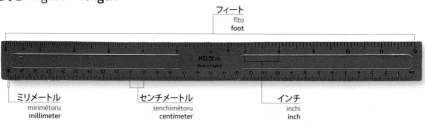

フィート
fito
foot

ミリメートル
mirimētoru
millimeter

センチメートル
senchimētoru
centimeter

インチ
inchi
inch

容量 yōryō • capacity

0.5リットル
rei ten go rittoru
half-liter

パイント
painto
pint

容積
yōseki
volume

ミリリットル
miririttoru
milliliter

計量カップ keiryō kappu | measuring cup

液体計量器 ekitai keiryōki
liquid measure

容器 yōki • container

紙パック
kami pakku
carton

包み
tsutsumi
package

瓶
bin
bottle

袋
fukuro
bag

カップ形容器
kappu-gata yōki | tub

広口瓶 hirokuchi bin | jar

缶
kan
can

缶詰容器 kanzume yōki | tin

霧吹き kirifuki | liquid dispenser

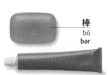

棒
bō
bar

チューブ
chūbu
tube

ロール
rōru
roll

パック
pakku
pack

スプレー缶
supurē kan
spray can

世界地図 sekai chizu ● **world map**

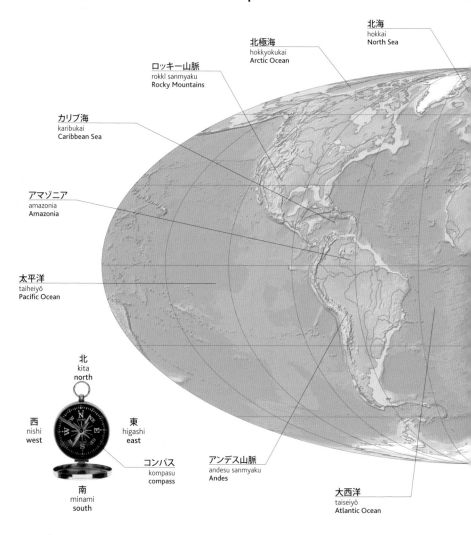

北海
hokkai
North Sea

北極海
hokkyokukai
Arctic Ocean

ロッキー山脈
rokkī sanmyaku
Rocky Mountains

カリブ海
karibukai
Caribbean Sea

アマゾニア
amazonia
Amazonia

太平洋
taiheiyō
Pacific Ocean

北
kita
north

西
nishi
west

東
higashi
east

コンパス
kompasu
compass

アンデス山脈
andesu sanmyaku
Andes

大西洋
taiseiyō
Atlantic Ocean

南
minami
south

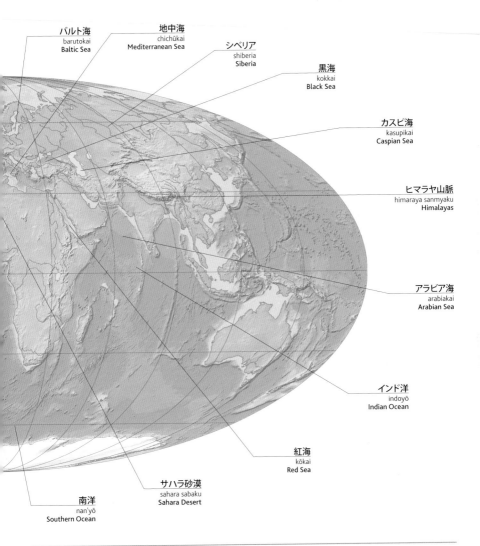

バルト海
barutokai
Baltic Sea

地中海
chichūkai
Mediterranean Sea

シベリア
shiberia
Siberia

黒海
kokkai
Black Sea

カスピ海
kasupikai
Caspian Sea

ヒマラヤ山脈
himaraya sanmyaku
Himalayas

アラビア海
arabiakai
Arabian Sea

インド洋
indoyō
Indian Ocean

紅海
kōkai
Red Sea

サハラ砂漠
sahara sabaku
Sahara Desert

南洋
nan'yō
Southern Ocean

日本語 nihongo • english

北米と中米 hokubei to chūbei • **North and Central America**

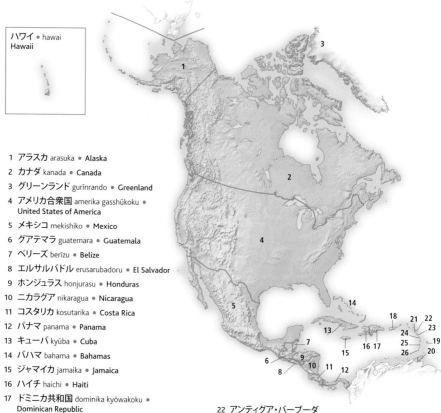

ハワイ • hawai
Hawaii

1 アラスカ arasuka • **Alaska**

2 カナダ kanada • **Canada**

3 グリーンランド gurīnrando • **Greenland**

4 アメリカ合衆国 amerika gasshūkoku •
United States of America

5 メキシコ mekishiko • **Mexico**

6 グアテマラ guatemara • **Guatemala**

7 ベリーズ berīzu • **Belize**

8 エルサルバドル erusarubadoru • **El Salvador**

9 ホンジュラス honjurasu • **Honduras**

10 ニカラグア nikaragua • **Nicaragua**

11 コスタリカ kosutarika • **Costa Rica**

12 パナマ panama • **Panama**

13 キューバ kyūba • **Cuba**

14 バハマ bahama • **Bahamas**

15 ジャマイカ jamaika • **Jamaica**

16 ハイチ haichi • **Haiti**

17 ドミニカ共和国 dominika kyōwakoku •
Dominican Republic

18 プエルトリコ puerutoriko • **Puerto Rico**

19 バルバドス barubadosu • **Barbados**

20 トリニダード・トバゴ torinidādo tobago •
Trinidad and Tobago

21 セントクリストファー・ネーヴィス sentokurisutofā nēvisu •
St. Kitts and Nevis

22 アンティグア・バーブーダ
antigua bābūda • **Antigua and Barbuda**

23 ドミニカ dominika • **Dominica**

24 セントルシア sentorushia • **St. Lucia**

24 セントビンセント及びグレナディーン諸島 sentobinsento
oyobi gurenadīn shotō • **St. Vincent and The Grenadines**

26 グレナダ gurenada • **Grenada**

南米 nambei • South America

1 ベネズエラ benezuera • **Venezuela**

2 コロンビア korombia • **Colombia**

3 エクアドル ekuadoru • **Ecuador**

4 ペルー perū • **Peru**

5 ガラパゴス諸島 garapagosu shotō • **Galapagos Islands**

6 ギアナ giana • **Guyana**

7 スリナム surinamu • **Suriname**

8 仏領ギアナ futsuryō giana • **French Guiana**

9 ブラジル burajiru • **Brazil**

10 ボリビア boribia • **Bolivia**

11 チリ chiri • **Chile**

12 アルゼンチン aruzenchin • **Argentina**

13 パラグアイ paraguai • **Paraguay**

14 ウルグアイ uruguai • **Uruguay**

15 フォークランド諸島 fōkurando shotō • **Falkland Islands**

関連用語 kanrenyōgo • vocabulary

国 kuni **country**	地方 chihō **province**	地帯 chitai **zone**
国家 kokka **nation**	領土 ryōdo **territory**	地区 chiku **district**
大陸 tairiku **continent**	植民地 shokuminchi **colony**	地域 chi'iki **region**
州 shū **state**	公国 kōkoku **principality**	首都 shuto **capital**

日本語 nihongo • english

ヨーロッパ yōroppa • Europe

1 アイルランド airurando • Ireland

2 英国 eikoku • United Kingdom

3 ポルトガル porutogaru • Portugal

4 スペイン supein • Spain

5 バレアレス諸島 barearesu shotō • Balearic Islands

6 アンドラ andora • Andorra

7 フランス furansu • France

8 ベルギー berugī • Belgium

9 オランダ oranda • Netherlands

10 ルクセンブルク rukusemburuku • Luxembourg

11 ドイツ doitsu • Germany

12 デンマーク denmāku • Denmark

13 ノルウェー noruwē • Norway

14 スウェーデン suwēden • Sweden

15 フィンランド finrando • Finland

16 エストニア esutonia • Estonia

17 ラトビア ratobia • Latvia

18 リトアニア ritoania • Lithuania

19 カリーニングラード karīningurādo • Kaliningrad

20 ポーランド pōrando • Poland

21 チェコ共和国 cheko kyōwakoku • Czech Republic

22 オーストリア ōsutoria • Austria

23 リヒテンシュタイン rihitenshutain • Liechtenstein

24 スイス suisu • Switzerland

25 イタリア itaria • Italy

26 モナコ monako • Monaco

27 コルシカ korushika • Corsica

28 サルディニア sarudinia • Sardinia

29 サンマリノ sanmarino • San Marino

30 バチカン市国 bachikan shikoku • Vatican City

31 シチリア shichiria • Sicily

32 マルタ maruta • Malta

33 スロベニア surobenia • Slovenia

34 クロアチア kuroachia • Croatia

35 ハンガリー hangarī • Hungary

36 スロバキア surobakia • Slovakia

37 ウクライナ ukuraina • Ukraine

38 ベラルーシ berarūshi • Belarus

39 モルドバ morudoba • Moldova

40 ルーマニア rūmania • Romania

41 セルビア serubia • Serbia

42 ボスニア・ヘルツェゴビナ bosunia herutsegobina • Bosnia and Herzegovina

43 アルバニア arubania • Albania

44 マケドニア makedonia • Macedonia

45 ブルガリア burugaria • Bulgaria

46 ギリシャ girisha • Greece

47 コソボ kosobo • Kosovo

48 モンテネグロ monteneguro • Montenegro

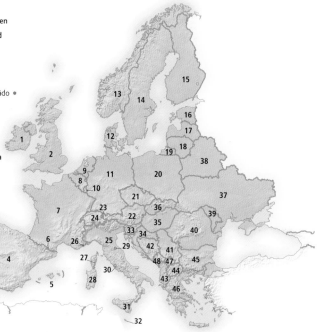

アフリカ afurika • Africa

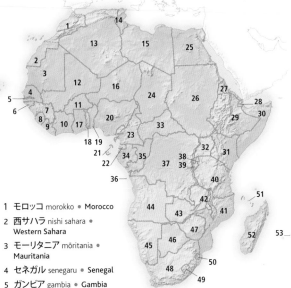

31 ケニア kenia • Kenya

32 ウガンダ uganda • Uganda

33 中央アフリカ共和国 chūō afurika kyōwakoku • Central African Republic

34 ガボン gabon • Gabon

35 コンゴ kongo • Congo

36 カビンダ kabinda • Cabinda

37 コンゴ民主共和国 kongo minshu kyōwakoku • Democratic Republic of the Congo

38 ルワンダ ruwanda • Rwanda

39 ブルンジ burunji • Burundi

40 モザンビーク mizambīku • Mozambique

41 タンザニア tanzania • Tanzania

42 マラウィ marawi • Malawi

43 ザンビア zambia • Zambia

44 アンゴラ angora • Angola

45 ナミビア namibia • Namibia

46 ボツワナ botsuwana • Botswana

47 ジンバブエ jimbabue • Zimbabwe

48 南アフリカ minami afurika • South Africa

49 レソト resoto • Lesotho

50 スワジランド suwajirando • Swaziland

51 コモロ komoro • Comoros

52 マダガスカル madagasukaru • Madagascar

53 モーリシャス mōrishasu • Mauritius

1 モロッコ morokko • Morocco

2 西サハラ nishi sahara • Western Sahara

3 モーリタニア mōritania • Mauritania

4 セネガル senegaru • Senegal

5 ガンビア gambia • Gambia

6 ギニアビサウ giniabisau • Guinea-Bissau

7 ギニア ginia • Guinea

8 シエラレオネ shiereareone • Sierra Leone

9 リベリア riberia • Liberia

10 コートジボワール kōtojibowāru • Ivory Coast

11 ブルキナファソ burukinafaso • Burkina Faso

12 マリ mari • Mali

13 アルジェリア arujeria • Algeria

14 チュニジア chunijia • Tunisia

15 リビア ribia • Libya

16 ニジェール nijēru • Niger

17 ガーナ gāna • Ghana

18 トーゴ tōgo • Togo

19 ベニン benin • Benin

20 ナイジェリア naijeria • Nigeria

21 サントメ・プリンシペ santome purinshipe • Sao Tome and Principe

22 赤道ギニア sekidō ginia • Equatorial Guinea

23 カメルーン kamerūn • Cameroon

24 チャド chado • Chad

25 エジプト ejiputo • Egypt

26 スーダン sūdan • Sudan

27 エリトリア eritoria • Eritrea

28 ジブチ jipuchi • Djibouti

29 エチオピア echiopia • Ethiopia

30 ソマリア somaria • Somalia

アジア ajia • Asia

1 トルコ toruko • Turkey

2 キプロス kipurosu • Cyprus

3 ロシア連邦 roshia rempō • Russian Federation

4 グルジア gurujia • Georgia

5 アルメニア arumenia • Armenia

6 アゼルバイジャン azerubaijan • Azerbaijan

7 イラン iran • Iran

8 イラク iraku • Iraq

9 シリア shiria • Syria

10 レバノン rebanon • Lebanon

11 イスラエル isuraeru • Israel

12 ヨルダン yorudan • Jordan

13 サウジアラビア saujiarabia • Saudi Arabia

14 クウェート kuwēto • Kuwait

15 バーレーン bārēn • Bahrain

16 カタール katāru • Qatar

17 アラブ首長国連邦 arabu shuchō-koku rempō • United Arab Emirates

18 オマーン omān • Oman

19 イエメン iemen • Yemen

20 カザフスタン kazafusutan • Kazakhstan

21 ウズベキスタン uzubekisutan • Uzbekistan

22 トルクメニスタン torukumenisutan • Turkmenistan

23 アフガニスタン afuganisutan • Afghanistan

24 タジキスタン tajikisutan • Tajikistan

25 キリギスタン kirigisutan • Kyrgyzstan

26 パキスタン pakisutan • Pakistan

27 インド indo • India

28 モルディブ morudibu • Maldives

29 スリランカ suriranka • Sri Lanka

30 中国 chūgoku • China

31 モンゴル mongoru • Mongolia

32 北朝鮮 kita chōsen • North Korea

33 韓国 kankoku • South Korea

34 日本 nihon • Japan

35 ネパール nepāru • Nepal

36 ブータン būtan • Bhutan

37 バングラデシュ banguradeshu • Bangladesh

38 ビルマ（ミャンマー）biruma (myanmā) • Myanmar

39 タイ tai • Thailand

40 ラオス raosu • Laos

41 ベトナム betonamu • Viet Nam

42 カンボジア kambojia • Cambodia

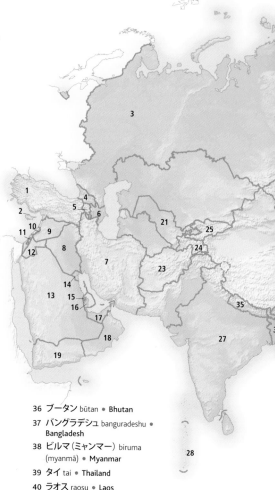

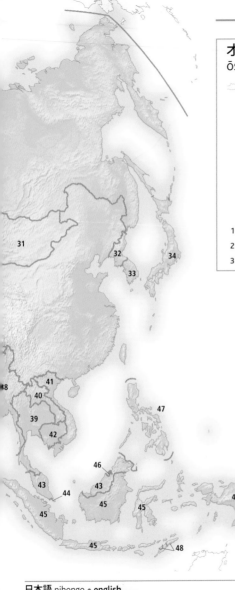

オーストラレーシア
ōsutorarēshia • Australasia

1　オーストラリア ōsutoraria • Australia
2　タスマニア tasumania • Tasmania
3　ニュージーランド nyūjīrando • New Zealand

43　マレーシア marēshia • Malaysia
44　シンガポール shingapōru • Singapore
45　インドネシア indoneshia • Indonesia
46　ブルネイ burunei • Brunei
47　フィリピン firipin • Philippines
48　東ティモール higashi timōru • East Timor
49　パプアニューギニア papuanyūginia • Papua New Guinea
50　ソロモン諸島 soromon shotō • Solomon Islands
51　バヌアツ banuatsu • Vanuatu
52　フィジー fijī • Fiji

不変化詞と反義語 fuhenkashi to hangigo ●
particles and antonyms

... へ
... e
to ...

...から
... kara
from ...

...から離れて
... kara hanarete
away from...

...に向かって
... ni mukatte
toward ...

...の上方
... no jōhō
over ...

...の下方
... no kahō
under ...

...に沿って
... ni sotte
along ...

...を横切って
... o yokogitte
across ...

...の前
... no mae
in front of ...

...の後ろ
... no ushiro
behind ...

...と一緒に
... to issho ni
with ...

...なしで
... nashi de
without ...

...の上へ
... no ue e
onto ...

...の中へ
... no naka e
into ...

...以前
... izen
before ...

...以後
... igo
after ...

中
naka
in

外
soto
out

...までに
... made ni
by ...

...まで
... made
until ...

真上
maue
above

真下
mashita
below

早い
hayai
early

遅い
osoi
late

内側
uchigawa
inside

外側
sotogawa
outside

今
ima
now

後ほど
nochihodo
later

上へ
ue e
up

下へ
shita e
down

いつも
itsumo
always

決して...ない
kesshite ... nai
never

...で
... de
at ...

...の向こう
... no mukō
beyond ...

頻繁に
himpan ni
often

稀に
mare ni
rarely

...を通って
... o tōtte
through ...

...を回って
... o mawatte
around ...

昨日
kinō
yesterday

明日
ashita
tomorrow

...の上
... no ue
on top of ...

...の側
... no soba
beside ...

最初
saisho
first

最後
saigo
last

...の間
... no aida
between ...

...の向かい側
... no mukaigawa
opposite ...

あらゆる
arayuru
every

いくつかの
ikutsuka no
some

近い
chikai
near

遠い
tōi
far

およそ
oyoso
about

丁度
chōdo
exactly

ここ
koko
here

あそこ
asoko
there

少し
sukoshi
a little

沢山
takusan
a lot

大きい ōkī **large**	小さい chīsai **small**	熱い atsui **hot**	冷たい tsumetai **cold**
幅の広い haba no hiroi **wide**	幅の狭い haba no semai **narrow**	開いた hiraita **open**	閉まった shimatta **closed**
背の高い se no takai **tall**	背の低い se no hikui **short**	満ちた michita **full**	空の kara no **empty**
高い takai **high**	低い hikui **low**	新しい atarashī **new**	古い furui **old**
厚い atsui **thick**	薄い usui **thin**	明るい akarui **bright**	暗い kurai **dark**
軽い karui **light**	重い omoi **heavy**	簡単な kantan na **easy**	難しい muzukashī **difficult**
硬い katai **hard**	柔らかい yawarakai **soft**	空き aki **free**	使用中 shiyō-chū **occupied**
湿った shimetta **wet**	乾いた kawaita **dry**	強い tsuyoi **strong**	弱い yowai **weak**
良い yoi **good**	悪い warui **bad**	太い futoi **fat**	細い hosoi **thin**
速い hayai **fast**	ゆっくりした yukkurishita **slow**	若い wakai **young**	老いた oita **old**
正しい tadashī **correct**	誤った ayamatta **wrong**	より良い yori yoi **better**	もっと悪い motto warui **worse**
きれいな kirei na **clean**	汚い kitanai **dirty**	黒 kuro **black**	白 shiro **white**
美しい utsukushī **beautiful**	醜い minikui **ugly**	面白い omoshiroi **interesting**	つまらない tsumaranai **boring**
高価な kōka na **expensive**	安い yasui **cheap**	病気の byōki no **sick**	健康な kenkō na **well**
静かな shizuka na **quiet**	うるさい urusai **noisy**	始め hajime **beginning**	終わり owari **end**

便利な表現 benri na hyōgen • useful phrases

基本的表現
kihonteki hyōgen
• essential phrases

はい
hai
Yes

いいえ
īe
No

多分
tabun
Maybe

どうぞ
dōzo
Please

ありがとう
arigatō
Thank you

どういたしまして
dō itashimashite
You're welcome

すみません
sumimasen
Excuse me

ごめんなさい
gomen nasai
I'm sorry

...しないでください
... shinaide kudasai
Don't ...

オーケー
ōkē
OK

それで結構です
sorede kekkō desu
That's fine

そうです
sōdesu
That's correct

違います
chigaimasu
That's wrong

挨拶 aisatsu •
greetings

もしもし
moshimoshi
Hello (on telephone)

さようなら
sayōnara
Goodbye

おはようございます
ohayō gozaimasu
Good morning

こんにちは
konnichiwa
Good afternoon

こんばんは
kombanwa
Good evening

おやすみなさい
oyasuminasai
Good night

お元気ですか
o-genki desuka
How are you?

私は...です
watashi wa ... desu
My name is...

お名前は何ですか
o-namae wa nan desuka?
What is your name?

彼/彼女のお名前は
kare/kanojo no o-namae wa?
What is his/her name?

...をご紹介します
... o go-shōkai shimasu
May I introduce...

こちらは...です
kochira wa ... desu
This is...

初めまして
hajimemashite
Pleased to meet you

また後で
mata ato de
See you later

標識 hyōshiki • signs

観光案内所
kankō annai-jo
Tourist information

入口
iriguchi
Entrance

出口
deguchi
Exit

非常口
hijōguchi
Emergency exit

押す
osu
Push

危険
kiken
Danger

禁煙
kin'en
No smoking

故障中
koshōchū
Out of order

開館時間
kaikan jikan
Opening times

入場無料
nyūjō muryō
Free admission

全日営業
zennichi eigyō
Open all day

割引料金
waribiki ryōkin
Reduced price

特売
tokubai
Sale

ノックしてください
nokku shite kudasai
Knock before entering

芝生立ち入り禁止
shibafu tachi'iri kinshi
Keep off the grass

援助 enjo • help

助けてください
tasukete kudasai
Please help me

分かりません
wakarimasen
I don't understand

知りません
shirimasen
I don't know

英語/日本語を話せますか
eigo/nihongo o
hanasemasuka?
Do you speak English/
Japanese?

英語を話せます
eigo hanasemasu
I speak English

スペイン語を話せます
supeingo o hanasemasu
I speak Spanish

もっとゆっくり言ってください
motto yukkuri itte kudasai
Please speak more slowly

書いてください
kaite kudasai
Please write it down for me

...をなくしました
... o nakushimashita
I have lost...

道案内 michi annai •
directions

道に迷いました
michi ni mayoimashita
I am lost

...はどこですか
... wa doko desuka?
Where is the...?

最寄りの...はどこですか
moyori no ... wa doko
desuka?
Where is the nearest...?

お手洗いはどこですか
o-tearai wa doko desuka?
Where are the toilets?

右です
migi desu
To the right

左です
hidari desu
To the left

まっすぐです
massugu desu
Straight ahead

...は、どのくらい離れていますか
... wa donokurai hanarete
imasuka
How far is...?

...への行き方を教えてください
... e no ikikata o oshiete
kudasai
How do I get to...?

道路標識 dōro hyōshiki
• road signs

注意
chūi
Caution

進入禁止
shinnyū kinshi
No entry

スピード落せ
supīdo otose
Slow down

迂回路
ukairo
Diversion

右側通行
migigawa tsūkō
Keep to the right

高速道路
kōsokudōro
Motorway

駐車禁止
chūsha kinshi
No parking

通行禁止
tsūkō kinshi
No through road

道路工事中
dōro kōji-chū
Roadworks

一方通行
ippōtsūkō
One-way street

譲れ
yuzure
Give way

止まれ
tomare
Stop

屈折あり
kussetsu ari
Dangerous bend

宿泊 shukuhaku •
accomodation

予約してあります
yoyaku shite arimasu
I have a reservation

朝食は何時ですか
chōshoku wa nanji
desuka
What time is breakfast?

食堂はどこですか
shokudō wa doko desuka?
Where is the dining room?

私の部屋は...号室です
watashi no heya wa
...-gōshitsu desu
My room number is...

...時に戻ります
... ji ni modorimasu
I'll be back at...o'clock

飲食 inshoku •
eating and drinking

乾杯!
kampai
Cheers!

美味しい/不味いです
oishī/mazui desu
It's delicious/awful

お酒は飲めません
o-sake wa nomemasen
I don't drink

煙草は吸いません
tabako wa suimasen
I don't smoke

肉は食べません
niku wa tabemasen
I don't eat meat

もう結構です
mō kekkō desu
No more for me, thank you

もう少し、いただけますか
mō sukoshi itadakemasuka?
May I have some more?

会計をお願いします
kaikei o onegaishimasu
Please give us the bill

領収書をください
ryōshūsho o kudasai
Please give us a receipt

禁煙席
kin'en seki
No-smoking area

健康 kenkō •
health

体調が優れません
taichō ga suguremasen
I don't feel well

気分が悪いです
kibun ga warui desu
I feel sick

最寄りの医者の電話番号は何ですか
moyori no isha no
denwabangō wa nan desuka?
What is the telephone
number of the nearest
doctor?

ここが痛いです
koko ga itai desu
It hurts here

熱があります
netsu ga arimasu
I have a temperature

妊娠...ヶ月です
ninshin ...-kagetsu desu
I'm...months pregnant

...の処方箋をください
... no shohōsen o kudasai
I need a prescription for...

普段は...を飲みます
fudan wa ... o nomimasu
I normally take ...

...にアレルギーがあります
... ni arerugī ga arimasu
I'm allergic to ...

大丈夫ですか
daijōbu desuka?
Will he/she be all right?

日本語索引 nihongo sakuin • Japanese index

日本語索引

日本語索引

日本語索引

英語索引 eigo sakuin • English index

english

A

à la carte 152
abdomen 12
abdominals 16
above 320
abseiling 248
acacia 110
accelerator 200
access road 216
accessories 36, 38
accident 46
account number 96
accountant 97, 190
accounts department 175
accused 180
ace 230, 273
Achilles tendon 16
acorn squash 125
acquaintance 24
acquitted 181
across 320
acrylic paints 274
actions 237, 229, 227, 233,
183
activities 263, 245, 162, 77
actor 254, 191
actors 179
actress 254
acupressure 55
acupuncture 55
Adam's apple 19
add v 165
address 98
adhesive tape 47
adjustable spanner 80
admissions 168
admitted 48
aduki beans 131
adult 23
advantage 230
adventure 255
advertisement 269
aerate v 91
aerobics 251
Afghanistan 318
Africa 317
after 320
afternoon 305
aftershave 73
aftersun 108
agate 289
agenda 174
aikido 236
aileron 210
air bag 201
air conditioning 200
air cylinder 239
air filter 202, 204
air letter 98
air mattress 267
air stewardess 190
air supply 199
air vent 210

aircraft 210
aircraft carrier 215
airliner 210, 212
airport 212
aisle 106, 168, 210, 254
alarm clock 70
Alaska 314
Albania 316
alcoholic drinks 145
alfalfa 184
Algeria 317
allergy 44
alley 298
alligator 293
allspice 132
almond 129
almond oil 134
almonds 151
along 320
alpine 87
alpine skiing 247
alternating current 60
alternative therapy 54
alternator 203
altitude 211
aluminum 289
Amazonia 312
ambulance 94
American football 220
amethyst 288
amniocentesis 52
amniotic fluid 52
amount 96
amp 60
amphibians 294
amplifier 268
anchor 214, 240
Andes 312
Andorra 316
anesthesiologist 48
angle 164
angler 244
Angola 317
angry 25
animals 292, 294
animated film 255
ankle 13, 15
ankle-length 34
anniversary 26
annual 86, 307
anorak 31, 33
answer 163
answer v 99, 163
answering machine 99
ant 295
antenna 295
antifreeze 199, 203
Antigua and Barbuda 314
antique shop 114
antiseptic 47
antiseptic wipe 47
antiwrinkle 41

antler 291
apartment building 59, 298
apéritif 153
aperture dial 270
apex 165
appeal 181
appearance 30
appendix 18
applaud v 255
apple 126
apple corer 68
apple juice 149
appliances 66
application 176
appointment 45, 175
apricot 126
April 306
apron 30, 50, 69, 212
aquamarine 288
Arabian Sea 313
arable farm 183
arborio rice 130
arc 164
arch 15, 85, 301
archery 249
architect 190
architecture 300
architrave 301
Arctic Circle 283
Arctic Ocean 312
area 165, 310
areas 299
arena 243
Argentina 315
arithmetic 165
arm 13
armband 238
armchair 63
Armenia 318
armpit 13
armrest 200, 210
aromatherapy 55
around 320
arrangements 111
arrest 94
arrivals 213
arrow 249
art 162
art college 169
art deco 301
art gallery 261
art nouveau 301
art shop 115
artery 19
artichoke 124
artist 274
arts and crafts 274, 276
arugula 123
ash 283
ashtray 150
Asia 318
assault 94

assistant 24
assisted delivery 53
asteroid 280
asthma 44
astigmatism 51
astronaut 281
astronomy 281
asymmetric bars 235
at 320
athlete 234
Atlantic Ocean 312
atmosphere 282, 286
atrium 104
attachment 177
attack 220
attack zone 224
attend v 174
attic 58
attractions 261
auburn 39
audience 254
August 306
aunt 22
aurora 286
Australasia 319
Australia 319
Austria 316
autocue 179
automatic 200
automatic door 196
autumn 31, 307
avalanche 247
avenue 299
avocado 128
awning 148
ax 95
axle 205
ayurveda 55
Azerbaijan 318

B

baby 23, 30
baby bath 74
baby care 74
baby carriage 75
baby changing facilities 104
baby monitor 75
baby products 107
baby sling 75
babygro 30
back 13
back brush 73
back seat 200
backboard 226
backdrop 254
backgammon 272
backhand 231
backpack 31, 37, 267
backstroke 239
backswing 233
bacon 118, 157
bad 321
badge 94

badminton 231
bag 311
bagel 139
baggage claim 213
baggage trailer 212
bags 37
baguette 138
Bahamas 314
bail 181
bait 244
bait v 245
bake v 67, 138
baked 159
baker 139
baker's 114
bakery 107, 138
baking 69
baking tray 69
balance wheel 276
balcony 59, 254
bald 39
bale 184
Balearic Islands 316
ball 15, 75, 221, 224, 226,
228, 230
ballboy 231
ballet 255
balsamic vinegar 135
Baltic Sea 313
bamboo 86,122
banana 128
bandage 47
Bangladesh 318
banister 59
bank 96, 284
bank charge 96
bank manager 96
bank transfer 96
bar 150, 152, 250, 256,
311
bar code 106
bar counter 150
bar mitzvah 26
bar snacks 151
bar stool 150
barb 244
Barbados 314
barbecue 267
barber 39, 188
bark 296
barley 130, 184
barman 191
barn 182
baroque 301
bars 74
bartender 150
basalt 288
base 164, 229
base station 99
baseball 228
baseline 230
baseman 228
basement 58

english

english

english

english

english

english

english

english

english

english

english

english

english

日本語 nihongo · english